U0424712

职业院校学生综合能力训练教材

口 语 轻 松 学

主　编　陈琴兰　吴亚萍

苏 州 大 学 出 版 社

图书在版编目(CIP)数据

口语轻松学/陈琴兰,吴亚萍主编. —苏州: 苏州大学出版社,2017.7
职业院校学生综合能力训练教材
ISBN 978-7-5672-2158-1

Ⅰ.①口… Ⅱ.①陈… ②吴… Ⅲ.①英语-口语-中等专业学校-教材 Ⅳ.①H319.32

中国版本图书馆 CIP 数据核字(2017)第 163409 号

书　　名: 口语轻松学

主　　编: 陈琴兰　吴亚萍
责任编辑: 金莉莉
装帧设计: 刘　俊

出版发行: 苏州大学出版社(Soochow University Press)
社　　址: 苏州市十梓街 1 号　**邮编**: 215006
印　　装: 丹阳市兴华印刷厂
网　　址: www.sudapress.com
邮购热线: 0512-67480030
销售热线: 0512-65225020

开　　本: 787mm×1092mm　1/16　**印张**: 10.5　**字数**: 243 千
版　　次: 2017 年 7 月第 1 版
印　　次: 2017 年 7 月第 1 次印刷
书　　号: ISBN 978-7-5672-2158-1
定　　价: 28.00 元

《口语轻松学》编委会

顾　问　王志强　尹为国　凌洪斌

主　编　陈琴兰　吴亚萍

副主编　许生如　周　君　陈修勇　李广洲

编　者　吴中美　赵　刚　马　群　卜长翠
魏海燕　周杨梅　张怀秀　张　鸣
葛振娣　李　娟

前言

《口语轻松学》是针对现有职业类学生英语教材内容、难度、要求等方面多样化的特点，结合各专业学生的学科需要而编写的提高职业类学生英语综合素质的教材。

本教材的设计思路：在九年义务制教育的基础上，以“了解语言知识→掌握语言技能→实际应用语言”为主线，以有关学生学习、生活及工作等话题为载体，激发学生学习英语的兴趣，掌握学习英语的策略，树立学好英语的信心，从而培养学生跨文化交际的意识，提高学生口语表达的能力，提升学生人文道德的素养。

全书共7个模块、29个话题。每个模块的编写力争体现中等职业学校英语课程的教学目标。语言贴近学生的实际生活和未来的发展目标，实用且有较强的时代气息。内容符合中职学生的认知规律和语言学习规律。活动和场景的设置形式多样，图文并茂。

本教材主要提供给一线教师用于英语口语教学和实践活动。教师可以通过一学年的系统教学，提高学生的英语交际能力，帮助学生正确认识和处理学习、生活和工作中遇到的各类交际问题。通过将语言知识的学习和语言技能的掌握相结合，将教师英语语言的教学和学生的人文素养的形成相结合，提高学生的英语口语水平及整体素质，促进学院素质教育的建设。

非常感谢学院各位领导和同仁在本教材编写过程中的悉心指导和大力协助。由于编者水平有限，加之时间仓促，书中难免有欠妥之处，恳请大家批评指正。

教材编写组

2017年3月

Contents

Module 1

Say You, Say Me

Say You, Say Me

Say you, say me 说出你自己，说出我自己
say it for always 应该永远是这样
that's the way it should be 本来就该是这样
say you, say me 说出你自己，说出我自己
say it together, naturally 大家一起自然地说出来
I had a dream, I had an awesome dream 我做了一个梦，一个可怕的梦
people in the park 人们在露天的公园里
playing games in the dark 在黑暗中玩着游戏
and what they played was a masquerade 他们玩的那个游戏是假面舞会
but from behind the walls of doubt 但从猜疑的墙壁后面
a voice was crying out 一个声音在大喊
say you, say me 说出你自己，说出我自己
say it for always 应该永远是这样
that's the way it should be 本来就该是这样
say you, say me 说出你自己，说出我自己
say it together, naturally 大家一起自然地说出来
as we go down life's lonesome highway 我们现在走在人生寂寞的高速路上
seems the hardest thing to do 似乎在这孤独的生命旅程中
is to find a friend or two 最难的就是找到一两个知己
their helping hand—someone who understands 他们理解你并向你伸出援助之手
and when you feel you've lost your way 当你感到空虚和迷茫时
you've got someone there to say 他们会在那里对你说
I'll show you oo, oo, oo 我给你指引
say you, say me 说出你自己，说出我自己

say it for always 应该永远是这样
that's the way it should be 本来就该是这样
say you, say me 说出你自己，说出我自己
say it together, naturally 大家一起自然地说出来
so you think you know the answers 也许你认为你知道了答案
oh no! 不，不
well the whole world's got ya dancing 整个世界正在变得越来越疯狂
that's right I'm telling you 这正是我要告诉你的
it's time to start believing 现在是开始重新建立信任的时候
oh yes! 噢，是的
believe in who you are 相信你自己
you are a shining star 你自己就是一颗闪耀的星
say you, say me 说出你自己，说出我自己
say it for always 应该永远是这样
that's the way it should be 本来就该是这样
say you, say me 说出你自己，说出我自己
say it together, naturally 大家一起自然地说出来
say it together, naturally 大家一起自然地说出来

Section 1 Greetings and Introductions

Warming-up

1. Match the common greetings with the correct pictures.

A. cheek kissing	B. hug	C. Cheers!	D. shake hands
E. kiss on the forehead	F. bow	G. rub noses	H. Good evening.

a. ______

b. ______

c. ______

d. 

e. ________________

f. ________________

g. ________________

h. ________________

2. *Work in pairs as follows.*

A: Jack, I would like to introduce you to my new friend Li Lei.

B: How do you do? …

Sentence Patterns

A	B
Good morning/afternoon/evening/night.	Thank you. Everything goes all right.
Hello. How is it going?	How do you do?
Nice to meet you.	Good morning/afternoon/evening …
How do you do?	My name is Jane. I'm from America.
What's your name, please?	Nice to meet you too.

Communicating

Dialogue A

(*Mr. Brown introduces Amy to Tom. Amy and Tom greet each other.*)

Mr. Brown: Good morning.

Tom: Good morning.

Mr. Brown: This is Amy Green. She is from France. She is a doctor. Amy, this is Tom. He is an American.

Tom: How do you do? Nice to meet you.

Amy Green: How do you do? Nice to meet you too.

Mr. Brown: And this is Jim. He comes from England.

Jim: How do you do?

Amy Green and Tom: How do you do?

Dialogue B

(*Amy and Julia are making greetings.*)

Amy: Hello! My name is Amy. What's your name?

Julia: Hi! My name's Julia.

Amy: Are you French too?

Julia: No, I'm not.

Amy: Where are you from?

Julia: I'm Swedish. I am from Sweden.

Amy: What do you do?

Julia: I'm a physicist.

Vocabulary

cheek	[tʃiːk]	*n.*	脸颊,脸蛋
forehead	[ˈfɔːhed]	*n.*	额; 前部
bow	[bəʊ]	*vi.*	(向……)弯腰,鞠躬
France	[frɑːns]	*n.*	法国,法兰西
England	[ˈɪŋglənd]	*n.*	英格兰
French	[frentʃ]	*n.*	法国人;法语
Swedish	[ˈswiːdɪʃ]	*n.*	瑞典人
Sweden	[ˈswɪdən]	*n.*	瑞典
physicist	[ˈfɪzɪsɪst]	*n.*	物理学家
How do you do?			你好。
Nice to meet you.			见到你很高兴。
come from (be from)			来自……
Where are you from?			你来自哪里?(你是哪国人?)

Practice

1. Finish the following dialogue according to the Chinese.

提示：Jack 和 Mary 见面，互相问候，然后 Jack 把他的新朋友 Li Lei 介绍给 Mary，于是 Li Lei 和 Mary 在认识后相互问好。

Jack: Hello, Mary, I haven't seen you for a long time. ____________?

Mary: Fine, thank you. ____________?

Jack: Fine too. I'd like you to meet my new friend Li Lei. Will you?

Mary: ____________. Who is it?

Jack: Li Lei, come here. ____________ to introduce a lady. This is Mary. This is Li Lei.

Mary: How do you do?

Li Lei: ____________?

Mary: My name is Mary Brown. Just call me Mary. I'm from California.

2. Make up the rest of the dialogue according to the Chinese above.

Culture Corner

世界各国问候集锦

问候方式一：鞠躬

适用国家：日本、韩国

在日本和韩国，人们见面时通常要鞠躬，以示对别人的尊敬。日本人与比较熟悉的人见面，互相鞠躬，二三秒为宜；如果遇见好友，弯腰的时间要稍微长些；在遇到长辈的时候要等长辈抬头以后才可抬头，有时甚至要鞠躬很多次。

在日本，行鞠躬礼时一般不能说话，寒暄通常是在行礼之后。在正式严肃场合行礼时如果说话，对方会视为不敬。

问候方式二：拥抱

适用国家：俄罗斯、巴西等国

在俄罗斯、巴西等国，好朋友见面时经常是拥抱对方。拥抱时不能抱得太紧，否则会给对方造成不适。

问候方式三：握手

适用国家：美国、加拿大、墨西哥、埃及等国

在美国和加拿大，人们见面时要非常有力地握对方的手，但时间很短。而在墨西哥和

埃及，人们虽然也以握手的形式来问候对方，但时间要略长一些，温柔一些。

在马来西亚，两人见面时会双手交握（右手掌放入对方双手掌中）一下，双手微触额头一下，双手微触胸前一下。

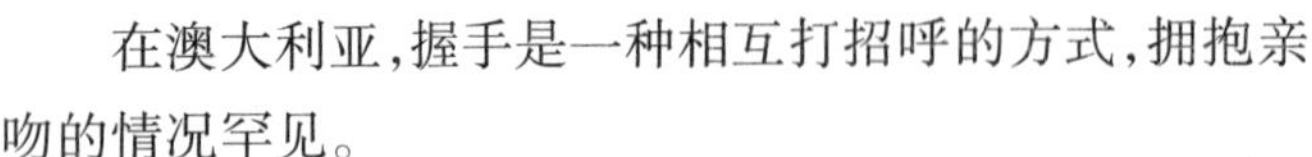

在澳大利亚，握手是一种相互打招呼的方式，拥抱亲吻的情况罕见。

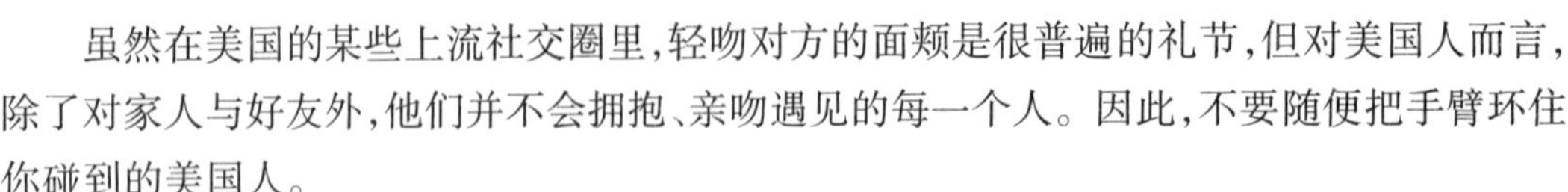

虽然在美国的某些上流社交圈里，轻吻对方的面颊是很普遍的礼节，但对美国人而言，除了对家人与好友外，他们并不会拥抱、亲吻遇见的每一个人。因此，不要随便把手臂环住你碰到的美国人。

问候方式四：把手放胸前

适用国家：泰国、印度尼西亚

泰国人对彼此及长辈打招呼时，会以双手合十，男性将双手放置于脸部前方，女性则置于胸前。印度尼西亚人碰到朋友或熟人的传统礼节是用右手按住胸口互相问好，对一般人则以握手问好。

问候方式五：碰鼻子

适用国家：印度、澳洲

印度人的问候方式是见面时以鼻额相碰，彼此紧紧拥抱。此外，澳洲毛利人喜欢碰鼻子行礼。

和印度人、毛利人见面前，记得先把鼻头上的黑头清理干净！

问候方式六：吐唾沫

适用国家：非洲某些部落

非洲通行的打招呼方式是举起右手，手掌向着对方，说明没有武器，表示友好。但有的部落有个礼节——吐唾沫，表示珍爱一个人或一件物品。当部落的战士第一次遇到小孩时，要朝他吐口唾沫。在触摸一件新武器时，要先在自己手上吐唾沫。这可能是一种古老的风俗，因为他们认为口水可以驱除邪恶。

问候方式七：伸舌头

适用国家：尼泊尔

尼泊尔主宾相见时，双手合十，口中道声“纳马斯得”（中文音译）。而在山区，主宾相见时，主人会伸出舌头，表示对客人的欢迎。因为舌头和心都是鲜红的，红舌头代表赤诚的心。

问候方式八：亲吻面颊

适用国家：意大利、法国、德国、西班牙等国

在意大利、西班牙和欧洲大部分国家，两个人打招呼的方式都是走上前快速地亲吻彼此的脸颊：先是右侧，然后左侧。如果彼此不太了解对方，也可以通过握手以示友好。这种

打招呼方式在大多数欧洲国家是一种惯例。

法国的亲吻礼仪比较复杂:先亲吻对方的右侧脸颊,亲吻的次数会因为不同的地区而有所差异,有些地区只吻一下,而在法国北部的大部分地区见面需要亲吻五下。

亲吻面颊在德国很常见,不过通常只是在脸颊左侧亲吻一下。一些德国斯多葛派人士和部分德国人最近呼吁废除这一见面习俗,他们认为亲吻面颊是异族文化入侵德国文化的一种表现。

英国民间见面亲吻的习俗很奇特,灵感可能源于他们周围的欧洲国家。你也可以坚持只和他握手。

荷兰的亲吻面颊礼仪是要按照脸颊右侧—左侧—右侧的顺序亲吻三下。关系一般的人之间以及两个男人之间是不会亲吻面颊的。

在希腊,熟人间以握手示友好,而亲近的人则是拥抱和亲吻。他们除了亲吻彼此脸颊两下以外,还伴着"拍手"一次,这样的方式使得他们的亲吻看起来更像是精心设计的一记"耳光"。

巴西女性之间亲吻面颊比男性要频繁得多,如在里约热内卢两个人打招呼要吻彼此脸颊两下,但官方统计的数据显示,在巴西不同的地区亲吻脸颊的次数从一次到三次不等。单身女性一般要亲吻三次,不过在某些地区,亲吻两次更常见。

南美人通常很敏感,新朋友之间亦是如此。一般见面就很随性地拥抱一下,然后在对方右侧脸颊亲吻一下。

各地人见面打招呼的方式不同,与不同国家的人们交往时要遵循一点:彼此尊重对方的文化和习惯,谨记入乡随俗。

Section 2 Likes and Dislikes

Warming-up

1. Look at the pictures below and work in pairs.

a. What do you know about the activities in the pictures?

b. Do you like them? Why or why not?

2. Work in pairs as follows.

A: What do you do in your spare time?

B: I like/love/enjoy ...

Sentence Patterns

Likes	Dislikes
I am interested in ...	I don't like ...
I like/love/enjoy ...	I really hate ...
I'm mad/crazy about ...	I don't care for ...
I prefer ...	I have no interest in ...
I am keen on ...	I don't think much of ...
... is my favourite.	I have a dislike of/for ...

Communicating

Dialogue A

(*Tom, a student, is talking with his classmate Lily.*)

Tom: Hi, Lily. What are you doing there?

Lily: I am making a kite.

Tom: Are you going to fly the kite?

Lily: Yes, I like flying kites when it is sunny but windy like today. What about you?

Tom: I don't really like flying kites. I prefer taking a walk in the hill.

Lily: So do I. Let's take a trip to the West Hill this Saturday.

Tom: That's great!

Dialogue B

(*Bruce is having a talk with his friend Lee.*)

Bruce: What do you like to do in your spare time?

Lee: I like to read in my free time.

Bruce: What kind of book do you like to read?

Lee: I like to read detective novels.

Bruce: Do you like to play sports?

Lee: Yes, I often play tennis and go bowling on the weekend.

Bruce: Which do you like better, playing tennis or going bowling?

Lee: I like both.

Vocabulary

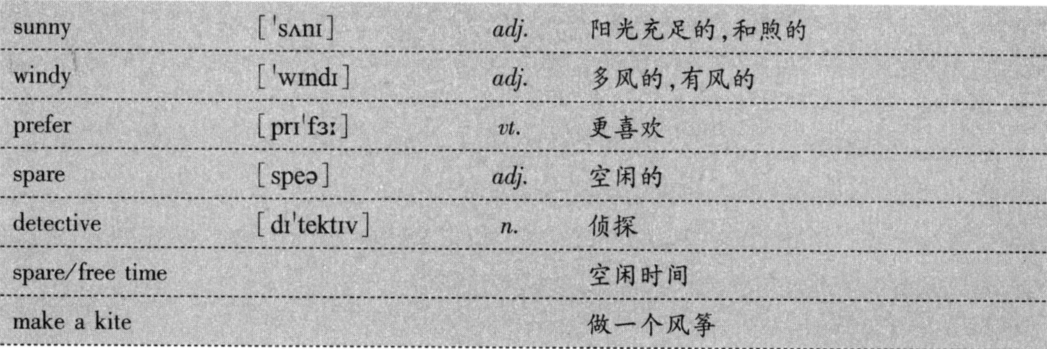

sunny	['sʌnɪ]	*adj.*	阳光充足的，和煦的
windy	['wɪndɪ]	*adj.*	多风的，有风的
prefer	[prɪ'fɜː]	*vt.*	更喜欢
spare	[speə]	*adj.*	空闲的
detective	[dɪ'tektɪv]	*n.*	侦探
spare/free time			空闲时间
make a kite			做一个风筝

fly kites	放风筝
take a trip	旅游
take a walk	散步
What about …	……怎么样?

Practice

1. Finish the following dialogue according to the Chinese.

提示:Mary 和 Helen 一起去餐厅吃饭。Helen 建议 Mary 吃点牛排,但是 Mary 更喜欢鸡肉和鱼,最后她们一起选了炸鸡和可乐。

Helen: Well, Mary, what would you like ____________? ____________ some steak?

Mary: Err … ____________ some chicken or fish.

Helen: Well, in that case, I'd recommend the fried chicken.

Mary: Yes, ____________.

Helen: I ____________ coca-cola, please.

2. Make up the rest of the dialogue according to the Chinese above.

Culture Corner

英美文化差异

如何表达自己的喜好?

英美人的思维模式是呈线性顺序进行演绎推理,而中国人则偏重于直观、直觉,多用意象思维方式。在跨文化语言交际中,这种不同表现在:英美人着眼于对客观事实的主观看法,中国人则着眼于对对方发出的信息或表明的态度做出直接反应。比如,对某一产品或某一设计,不管满意与否,英美人倾向于先给予赞扬,而中国人往往先挑剔。对来自对方的赞扬,中国人和英美人的反应也是不同的。英美人认为对方的赞扬是对自己某件事的认可,对待这种赞扬,英美人觉得应表达自己的谢意,所以通常用“Thank you”,“I'm glad to hear that”。而中国人觉得,谦逊是一种美德,得到他人赞赏时,经常表现出不好意思和受之有愧之感,往往会以“哪里,哪里”“过奖,过奖”“还差得很远”等作为回答,这会使英美人感到迷惑不解。

很多平日彬彬有礼的中国人,在与北美人交往时,并没有学会使用北美人的礼仪与特有的表达习惯,只是套用我们中国人的礼仪和表达方式去交往,以至于造成了不少人对中国文化缺乏了解。因此,一方面外国人需要多了解中华文化和礼仪;另一方面,我们自己也要了解一些外国人在交流时所特有的表达方式。

什么样的话太尖锐?

很多中国人与英美人交往的方式,是从外国电影里学来的。例如,当不同意某人的观点时,我们会发现电影里的人物,很多时候会大声地说"I object to it(我反对)""Absolutely no way(绝对不行)""Definitely not(绝对不是)"等。这些英文语句,本身并没有任何语法错误,甚至在国内的很多教科书中,也传授类似的表达方式。电影中出现类似的表达方式,是为了将人物戏剧化和情节冲突化,因为高度戏剧化和冲突化的电影,往往最会受到观众的喜爱,也才会有更多的票房收入。但是如果你生活在国外,你会发现外国人在一般情况下无论是对待朋友、同事、邻居还是陌生人,都不会轻易使用上述的类似语句。如果使用了会发生什么情况呢?使用者很可能会被英语是母语的人视为"极为粗暴无礼、缺乏基本教养、说话过于尖刻"而遭厌恶!英语中类似的表达方式最好别用。

你需要学会尊重别人,即使别人是你的对手。西方人说:"我虽然不同意你的观点,但是我要用我的生命去捍卫你表达思想的权利。"

如何委婉地拒绝?

世界上无论多么伟大多么完美的人,都拒绝过别人,也都被别人拒绝过。如果别人对你的要求说"不",他只是拒绝了你现在的要求而已。同样地,你想拒绝别人的要求,无论是合理的或者过分的要求,你都可以很有礼貌地说声"不"。英美人一般先说一些感谢的客套话,然后再拒绝;有时他们可能还需要给予必要的、简短的解释,既避免了过于唐突生硬,又能缓冲因拒绝带来的尴尬,尤其是对于那些喜欢和关心自己的人,或者别人是因为出于好心而提出建议。以下是表达不同意的部分技巧。

技巧1 直接而礼貌地说"不"。

老外:Do you think that you could help me practice my China?

(你能帮我练练我的中文吗?)

中国人:I'd really like to, but I am on such a tight schedule!

(我很愿意,但是我确实没时间。)

其他可以用来拒绝别人的句子。

· I'm sorry, but ... I already have plans for tonight.

(抱歉,但是今天晚上我已经有安排了。)

· I feel terrible, but ...

(我感到抱歉,但是……)

· I wish I could help you, but ...

(我希望我能帮你,但是……)

· I'd really like to, but ...

(我也希望如此,但是……)

如果你认为对方的要求,侵犯了你的个人隐私或利益,你可以这样回答:

· I'd rather not answer that, if you don't mind.

(如果你不介意的话,我宁愿不回答这个问题。)

· I'm very sorry but that question makes me uncomfortable.

(抱歉,但是那个问题使我感到不适。)

· That question is a little too personal. I'd rather not answer it.

(这个问题有点涉及个人隐私,我宁愿不回答。)

拒绝别人时,尽量还要避免以下的用语:

· Are you kidding? (你在开玩笑?)

· You must be crazy! (你一定疯了!)

技巧2 理解。先告诉对方自己理解对方的观点,然后再陈述自己的理由。

· I appreciate what you have to say, but …

(我感谢你陈述的观点,但是……)

· I can see where you are coming from. In my opinion, though …

(我理解你这样说的缘由,虽然我的意见是……)

技巧3 重复对方的观点,然后再提出你自己的观点,以便让对方确切地知道你的确知道了对方的观点,而并不只是嘴上说说而已。

· I can see why you think … Canadians are just like Americans. However, because I am Canadian, I would like to talk about some differences.

(我理解为什么你认为……加拿大人像美国人。但因为我是加拿大人,我愿意谈论一些我的不同的看法。)

· As you pointed out, China had been isolated for a long time, but that does not mean …

(正如你指出的那样,中国曾经很长时间与世界隔绝,但是那并不意味着……)

· I realize … that it is difficult not to stereotype other people, however …

(我意识到……不以刻板思维来衡量别人很难,然而……)

技巧4 弥补或者给予其他选择。

拒绝别人时,我们可以做出必要的解释,也可以给予别人以其他选择的机会。比如说“下次如何”,虽然这只是一种礼节上的回答,不一定“下一次”就怎么样,但是它向对方展示了你的好意,虽然这是一种拒绝。当然,与外国人在一起,如果你根本就不想有“下次”,也就没有必要给予对方选择的机会了,直接礼貌地拒绝就可以了。另外,在表达不同意时,说话者要尽可能在语气、语调和用词上,柔和、礼貌一些。所以表达不同意时,我们可以这样说:

· Don't you think it would be better …

(你不认为这样……更好一些吗?)

· Shouldn't we consider …

(我们难道不该考虑……)

· Oh, I am not so sure about that, because …

(噢,对此我不太肯定,因为……)

· I'm afraid I don't agree, because …

(我恐怕我不能同意,因为……)

· I'm sorry, but I have to disagree with you.

（我很抱歉，但是我有不同的观点）

最后，还是让我们回到开始的例子上吧。在例子中，因为那位中国人简短而干脆的拒绝，再加上没有运用正确的语音语调，让对方误认为那位中国人粗暴无礼。其实，我们完全可以这样直率而礼貌地回答：“我也非常希望能与你一起谈一谈。但是非常抱歉，我今天实在没有时间。让我们改天再畅谈一番好吗？”

Section 3 Farewell

Warming-up

1. Match the phrases with the correct pictures.

A. bye to school	B. bye to a single life	C. bye to bad habits
D. bye to friends	E. bye to my fans	F. bye to the family

a. ________________

b. ________________

c. ________________

d. ________________

e. ________________

f. ________________

2. Work in pairs as follows.

A: What do you think of Picture a?

B: It's …

Sentence Patterns

Expressing Farewell	Possible Responses
Goodbye.	Goodbye.
See you!	See you.
I'm afraid I must be leaving now.	Do you really want to go?
I'm afraid I have to go now.	Can't you stay any longer?
I think it's time for me to leave now.	Oh, see you then.

Communicating

Dialogue A

(*Tom is saying goodbye to Mary.*)

Tom: Well, I must go now. The plane is about to take off.

Mary: Yes, it's time to say goodbye now.

Tom: I'll miss you all the time.

Mary: Me too. And take care of yourself.

Dialogue B

(*John is to leave on Sunday afternoon.*)

John: I'm calling to say goodbye.

Jack: When are you off?

John: I'm going home on Sunday afternoon.

Jack: Well, goodbye. See you soon.

John: Please don't forget to say goodbye to your parents for me.

Vocabulary

miss	[mɪs]	*vt.*	想念,思念
take off			起飞
It's time to do sth.			该是做某事的时候了。
all the time			一直
take care of			照顾
be to do			即将做
forget to do sth.			忘记去做某事

◈ Practice

1. Finish the following dialogue according to the Chinese.

提示：Mike 要回美国了，他的朋友 Alice 来机场送行，他们都说会想念对方。Mike 很感谢 Alice 对他的诸多帮助。Alice 说能帮助多年的朋友她感到高兴！Mike 希望 Alice 有一天能去美国旅游。Alice 祝他回家旅途愉快，并请 Mike 代她向他家人问好。

Mike：It's very kind of you ____________________.

Alice：____________________. I'll miss you.

Mike：____________________. Thanks for ____________________.

Alice：We have been friends ____________________. I'm happy that I can help you.

2. Make up the rest of the dialogue according to the Chinese above.

◈ Culture Corner

（一）告别语的差异

中西语言中有多种不同的告别语。如在和病人告别时，中国人常说“多喝点开水”“多穿点衣服”“早点休息”之类的话，表示对病人的关怀。但西方人绝不会说这类话，因为这样说会被认为有指手画脚之嫌。他们会说“多保重”或“希望你早日康复”等。

一位美国人在和他的中国朋友告别时说：“我会保持联系。”可是这位中国朋友等了一年多也未见只言片语，便抱怨他不讲信用。其实，这句话仅仅是一种告别语，相当于“再见”，说话人并无他意，更没有做任何许诺。此外西方文化中如果客人想告别，通常要提前几分钟将告别的意思暗示或委婉地向主人表达，并征得同意，然后才可以离开。如果突然说“时间不早了”，随即站起来和主人告别，这在西方文化中被认为是不礼貌的。

（二）英国人道别的七大方式

英国人道别的表达方式是怎样的呢？

1. Goodbye. /Bye.

Goodbye 较为少用，通常用于绝对的道别（暗指将不会再见），而 bye 则是一种更放松、非正式的道别方法。

2. See you later. /See you.

3. It was nice to see you again.

这是向某个熟人道别时重要的表达方式之一。

4. Take care.

无论是正式还是非正式场合，跟朋友或陌生人，你都可以用这句话来表达真切的问候，道一声珍重。

5. Take it easy.

通常用于非正式场合。虽然很多人在劝别人“保持冷静”时会用上一句 Take it easy，但这种道别方式也传递着“我希望你有机会放松一下、享受当下”的意思。

6. Have a good one.

这是另外一种地道的道别方法，主要表达希望某人安好。你也可以说 Have a good day/weekend/trip/vacation，但 have a good one 表达的是广泛意义上的关切问候。

7. Until ...

这种表达方式不像它过去那么常见，当你知道自己将再见到某人，就可以这么说，如 Until tomorrow/Saturday（明天见/周六见）等。

Module 2

Auld Lang Syne

Auld Lang Syne

Should auld acquaintance be forgot, 怎能忘记旧日朋友,

and never brought to mind? 心中能不怀想?

Should auld acquaintance be forgot and days of auld lang syne, 旧日朋友岂能相忘, 友谊地久天长

For auld lang syne, my friends, 友谊万岁,我的朋友们,

For auld lang syne, 友谊万岁,

We'll take a cup o'kindness yet, 举杯痛饮同声歌颂,

For auld lang syne. 友谊地久天长。

Section 1 Friendship

Warming-up

1. Match the expressions with the correct pictures.

A. 患难见真情。 B. 和朋友走在黑暗中要好过一个人独自在光明中行走。

C. 没有朋友,世界成了荒野。 D. 人生在世无朋友,犹如生活无太阳。

E. 交朋友 F. 互相帮助 G. shake hands H. shoulder to shoulder

Making Friends

a. ______________

b. ______________

c. ______________

d. ______________

A friend in need
is a friend indeed.

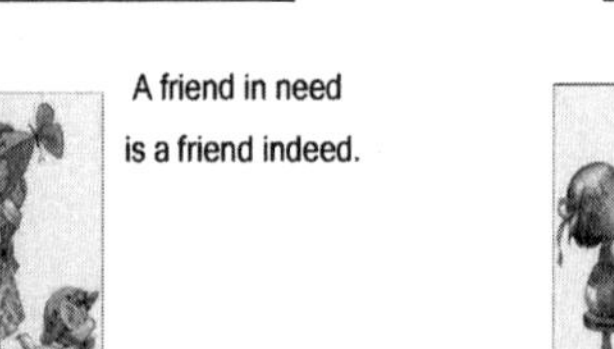

e. ______________

Without a friend,
the world is
a wilderness.

f. ______________

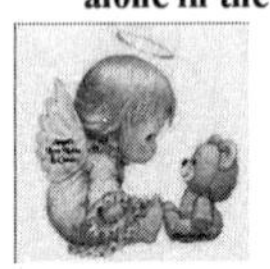

Walking with a friend in the dark is better than walking alone in the light.

g. ______________

Proverb
A life without a friend
is a life without a sun.

h. ______________

2. Work in pairs as follows.

A: What do you think of a good friend?

B: I think a good friend should (not) be ...

In my opinion, a good friend is someone who is (ordinary-looking, good-looking, handsome, pretty, beautiful, generous, strong, brave, friendly, kind, easy-going, honest, helpful, trusty, funny, loyal, smart, hard-working, wise, clever, warm-hearted, cool-headed, dutiful, happy, understanding, poor, rich, etc.)

Sentence Patterns

—I'm glad I have you for a friend. —Me too.
—I'm here if you need me. —Thanks. The same for you.
—I need to talk. Can you listen for(留心听) me? —Sure, I can listen.
—You're a friend who I can always trust/rely on/depend on/count on.
—I think friendship is love with understanding.
—Last night we had a big quarrel because she stood me up.
—We've known each other since we were toddlers.
—A good friend should be a good listener.
—A faithful and loyal friend is hard to find.
—A friend without faults will never be found.

◈ Communicating

Dialogue A

(*Jack and Joan are classmates. They are talking about what friendship standards are.*)

Jack: What kind of qualities do you look for in your friends?

Joan: I like to make friends with open and friendly people.

Jack: I like active and fun ones.

Joan: Maybe that's why a person always has different kinds of friends in his or her life.

Jack: Yes. I like to make friends with those who I can get along well with too. That's a great feeling.

Joan: I can't agree you more.

Dialogue B

(*After class, Jack and Joan go on talking about what friendship standards are.*)

Jack: Well, how long have you known Jimmy?

Joan: We've known each other since we were toddlers.

Jack: Really? He seems faithful and loyal.

Joan: What's wrong with you? Aren't you happy?

Jack: Last night I had a big quarrel with Lucy, because she stood me up.

Joan: You know, friendship is love with understanding. A friend without faults will never be found.

Jack: Thank you for your encouragement.

Joan: Don't mention it.

◈ Vocabulary

quality	[ˈkwɒlətɪ]	*n.*	质量,品质;特性
active	[ˈæktɪv]	*adj.*	积极的,活跃的
toddler	[ˈtɒdlə]	*n.*	学步的小孩
faithful	[ˈfeɪθfl]	*adj.*	忠实的,忠诚的;如实的;准确可靠的
loyal	[lɔɪəl]	*adj.*	忠诚的,忠心的,忠贞的
quarrel	[ˈkwɒr(ə)l]	*n.*	吵架;反目
understand	[ˌʌndəˈstænd]	*vi.*	理解;懂得;熟悉

fault	[fɔːlt]	n.	错误；缺点；毛病；故障；[地质]断层
encouragement	[ɪnˈkʌrɪdʒmənt]	n.	鼓励，激励，奖励
make friends with			交朋友
get along well with			与……相处融洽
I can't agree you more.			我完全赞同你的看法。
have a big quarrel with ...			和……大吵一架
stand someone up			让某人空等一场，失约，放某人鸽子

Practice

1. Choose the best answer from the box to complete the dialogue.

提示：Steve 和 Kevin 诉说自己因为放了别人鸽子而与对方发生了矛盾，心中苦恼该不该向他道歉，经过 Kevin 的鼓励，终于鼓起勇气愿意和对方道歉。

A. Why don't you say sorry to him?
B. I think the most important thing is your friendship.
C. What's the matter with you?
D. You know I'm always here for you, man.
E. Come on. I'm your best friend.

Kevin: You look unhappy, Steve. ____________

Steve: Eh, I don't know if I want to talk about it.

Kevin: ____________ You can talk to me about anything.

Steve: Well ... Last night we had a big quarrel because I stood him up. So he got angry with me.

Kevin: ____________

Steve: En ... I think so ... but ...

Kevin: Come on! ____________.

Steve: En ... thank you for your encouragement.

Kevin: Don't worry about it. ____________.

Steve: I really appreciate it.

Kevin: Anytime.

2. Finish the following dialogue according to the Chinese.

A: ____
____(你和 Jack 认识有多长时间)?

B: We've known each other since we were toddlers.

A: Really? ______________________________

______________________________(他看起来很有诚信,又很忠实).

B: Well, he is, but he can not be perfect all the time.

A: ______________________________(你什么意思)?

B: A friend without faults will never be found. I need to talk. Can you listen for me?

A: Sure, ______________________________(好朋友应该是能倾听的人).

B: Thanks. I'm glad I have you for a friend.

A: Me too. ______________________________(如果你需要我随时在这儿).

Culture Corner

(一) 美国人如何看待友谊

美国人虽然把友情看得重要,但没中国人看得那么重。举个简单的例子,在中国,朋友之间,可以随时牺牲一些自身利益来帮助对方;在美国,一般涉及个人利益时,美国人很难牺牲自己的利益去为对方做些什么。

当求助于美国朋友时,如果他们当时正在处理自己的事情,他们会很直接地告诉你NO;当然,如果没有什么要紧的事情做,他们也会很热情地过来帮忙。因此,对于美国人,直说就好,不用兜圈子。

(二) 变敌人为朋友

美国的RealNetworks公司曾经向美国联邦法院提起诉讼,指控比尔·盖茨的微软公司违反反垄断法,并要求其赔偿十亿美元。但在官司还没有结束的情况下,RealNetworks公司的首席执行官格拉塞却致电比尔·盖茨,希望得到微软的技术支持,以使自己的音乐文件能够在网络和便携设备上播放。所有的人都认为比尔·盖茨一定会拒绝他。但出人意料的是,比尔·盖茨对他的提议表现出出奇的欢迎。他通过微软的发言人表示,如果对方真的想要整合软件的话,他将很有兴趣合作。

众所周知,微软和苹果两大公司自20世纪80年代起就一直处于敌对状态。到了90年代中期,微软公司明显占据了领先优势,占领了约90%的市场份额,而苹果公司则举步维艰。但让所有人大跌眼镜的是,1997年,微软向苹果公司投资1.5亿美元,把苹果公司从倒闭的边缘拉了回来。2000年,微软为苹果推出Office 2001。自此,微软与苹果真正实现双赢,他们的合作伙伴关系进入了一个新时代。

常人不可理解的两件事都发生在世界首富比尔·盖茨身上。他的成功,源于很多因素,包括他对商机的把握以及天才的设计能力,但其中还包括他对对手所采取的态度。

Section 2 Making a Telephone Call

Warming-up

1. Have you seen the following telephones?

2. Can you tell us a story of one of them?

Sentence Patterns

Caller	Receiver
Hello! This is ... speaking. /Could(May) I speak to ...? /Is ... in?	Who's that speaking?/May I have your name?/Is that ...(speaking)?
I'm sorry I have the wrong number. I'm sorry to call you so late. May I leave a message?	Pardon? I can't catch what you are saying. Hold the line, please. I'll get him/her to phone.
Please connect me with extension two-one-one.(请帮我转分机211) I'm sorry. I'm afraid you've got the wrong number.	Would you speak more slowly?

Communicating

Dialogue A

(*Xiao Nan calls for Qiang Dong to play football.*)

Xiao Nan: Hello. May I speak to Qiang Dong?

Qiang Dong: This is Qiang Dong speaking. Who's that, please?

Xiao Nan: Hello, Qiang Dong. This is Xiao Nan, your classmate. It is Sunday and it is a fine day today. Let's go and play football in the new playground of our school, shall we?

Qiang Dong: Good idea. But where and what time shall we meet?

Xiao Nan: At the school gate and at 9:00 a.m.

Qiang Dong: OK. See you then, Xiao Nan.

Xiao Nan: See you.

Dialogue B

(*Today is Friday. It's time to go home for the weekend, so Hu Lili telephones Taxi Service.*)

A: Hello. Yizheng Taxi Service. How can I help you?

B: Hi. I'm calling to reserve a taxi. I need a cab to the city centre this Friday afternoon.

A: All right. Please give me your name, address and phone number.

B: Okay. My name is Hu Lili. My address is No. 2 Guyunhe Road, Yizheng Technician College. And my phone number is 13600079234.

A: Thanks. I got it. What time will you want us to pick you up?

B: 4 o'clock in the afternoon.

A: All right. Your cab will be at your school gate at 3:45 p.m. Thank you for your call.

Vocabulary

reserve	[rɪˈzɜːv]	*vt.*	预约;储备;保留
cab	[kæb]	*n.*	出租汽车
call for			要求;需要
Taxi Service			出租汽车服务
I got it.			我知道了。
pick sb. up			开车去接某人

Practice

1. Choose the best answer from the box to complete the dialogue.

A. That sounds great.
B. What are you doing there?
C. What about you?
D. I hope you will enjoy yourselves.
E. Who's that speaking?

A: Hello! ____________

B: This is Karen speaking.

A: Where are you going for your vacation?

B: I have no idea. ____________

A: I'm going to Sanya.

B: ____________

A: I am playing beach volleyball, eating seafood, and going sightseeing.

B: ____________ Who else is going with you?

A: My parents and my sister.

B: ____________

A: Thank you.

2. Finish the following dialogue according to the Chinese.

提示:张林先生(A)打电话给史密斯先生,史密斯先生外出,他的秘书(B)接听了电话。张林请她转告史密斯先生,回来给他回电。

A: Hello. ________________________________. Is Mr. Smith there?

B: I'm sorry, __________________ now. I'm his secretary. May I __________________ for him?

A: May I know when he will be back?

B: He won't be back until five.

A: Well, will you tell him ________________________ as soon as he gets in? My company name is Leon and my telephone number is 3608-0020.

B: All right. Mr. Zhang. I will give him your message.

A: ____________________. Goodbye.

◈ Culture Corner

西方电话常识及基本礼仪

在英美国家，几乎每家每户都装有电话，有的家庭甚至还装有几部电话。人们用电话这种快捷、廉价的通信方式安排约会、访友、做生意以及获得各种信息等。

另外，公用电话也随处可见。打公用电话时通常应事先准备好一些硬币，有5美分的(nickle)，有10美分的(dime)，以及25美分的(quarter)等。公用电话的使用方法大致为：先拿起话筒，然后将硬币投入电话收费孔中，待听到接通的响声后，便可拨号。若是电话不通，那么挂上话筒后，所投入的硬币从电话机下面的一个小孔退出。

值得注意的是，英美国家的电话号码与我国的电话号码有相同的地方，也有不同的地方：英国的电话号码通常由一个四位数的地区代码和(或)总机名称再加上三至七位的电话号码组成，如Oxford (0865)56767。地区代码也叫标准代码，在跨地区打电话时使用。在一些大城市，如伦敦，电话号码由两位数的地区代码和一个七位数的号码组成：01-2468022。

在美国以及加拿大，电话号码通常由一个三位数的地区代码和一个七位数号码组成。地区代码只在长途电话时才使用，在说或写电话号码时经常被省略掉。如果写上的话，它放在电话号码前的括号中。电话号码的前三位数与后四位数之间通常用一连字符分开，如(202)234-5678。

需要特别说明一下的是，由于各国文化和习俗方面的差异，打电话时各国也往往有各自的特殊做法和语言表达。在西方国家人们在接电话时往往先自报家门，如：

Hello, this is 213688. 喂,我这儿的电话号码是213688。

Hello, Jim speaking. 喂,我是吉姆。

在接电话时,你若发现对方拨错了号码或他要找的人不是你而是别人,你一般应再重复一次自己的电话号码或姓名,然后告诉对方:Sorry, you've dialed the wrong number(对不起,你拨错号码了),然后挂上电话。同样,若是自己拨错了号码,也应说声:Sorry, I've dialed the wrong number(对不起,我拨错号码了)。

由于打电话时双方彼此看不见,所以当一方在讲话时,听话一方往往用 Yes, Mm, Uhhuh, Right, I see 之类的词语来回应,表示自己正在听对方说话,这样以免得对方担心你没有在听。

最后值得注意的是,有些电话用语有一定的特殊性,不宜随便改变。比如,在电话中问 May I speak to Mr. Smith? 若接电话的正是 Mr. Smith, 那么他会说 This is Smith speaking, 或只说 Smith speaking, 甚至也可只说 Speaking, 都是指“我就是”或“我正是”,言外之意即你有什么事请讲。又如在电话中我们要问“你是哪位?”,一般不直接说 Who are you? 而说 Who's that (speaking)? 所有这些特殊的表达都要引起注意。

打电话时,我们需要注意以下三个方面的礼节。

一、选择好通话时间。应根据对方的工作时间、生活习惯选好打电话的时间。

比如,白天宜在早晨8点以后,节假日应在9点以后。晚间则应在22点以前,以免对方不在或打扰对方及其家人的休息。如无特殊情况,不宜在中午休息时和一日三餐的常规时间打电话,以免影响别人休息和用餐。

二、拟好通话要点。在电话中应该说些什么,一次电话该打多久,打电话前应有“腹稿”。如怕遗漏,可拟出通话要点,理顺说话的顺序,备齐与通话内容有关的文件和资料。

三、讲究通话语言艺术。话如其人,不管是在公司还是在其他地方,根据双方在电话里的讲话方式,就可以判断出对方的基本教养水准。电话的语言艺术,不仅要坚持用“您好”开头,“请”字在中,“谢谢”结尾,更重要的是控制语气语调。

Section 3 Giving an Invitation

Warming-up

1. Match the words or phrases with the correct pictures.

A. live CS B. picnic C. dancing
D. coffee drinking E. cinema F. badminton

a. ______________

b. ______________

c. ______________

d. ______________

e. ______________

f. ______________

2. Have you been invited to other activities besides the above? Can you write out 3 of them?

① ____________ ② ____________ ③ ____________

Sentence Patterns

Invitations	Responses
What are you doing tomorrow?	I'm free/busy tomorrow.
Are you busy tomorrow?	It's very kind of you. Thank you.
Would you like to come to my birthday party?	That would be a great idea.
We'd like to invite you to go shopping with us.	That's very kind of you, but I'm afraid …
Could I have the pleasure of dancing with you?	Sorry, but I can't. Thank you all the same.

(Continued)

Invitation	Response
I wonder if you would like to come around and have a meal sometimes.	Yes, I'm glad to.
What about Saturday evening?	Let's make it around six.

Communicating

Dialogue A

(*Joe wants to invite Mary to see a film.*)

Mary: Joe, how are you doing?

Joe: I am great! How about you, Mary?

Mary: I am doing great! Thank you for asking, Joe.

Joe: I am wondering if you want to go to see a movie with me tonight.

M: I need to stay at home tonight and finish my term paper.

Joe: OK. What about going to the movies on Friday night?

Mary: What do you plan on seeing?

Joe: I am thinking about seeing a war movie.

Mary: How about *Captain America 2*?

Joe: That's a blockbuster.

Dialogue B

(*Joe wants to invite Mary and her daughter for dinner.*)

Joe: When can we expect you and your daughter for dinner? Next Saturday?

Mary: Next Saturday? I'm sorry. I've promised to go to a Chinese opera with my daughter.

Joe: How about Sunday then?

Mary: Sunday sounds fine. What time?

Joe: Does 6:30 suit you?

Mary: It suits us. We'll see you then.

Vocabulary

captain	[ˈkæptɪn]	*n.*	队长,首领;船长;上尉;海军上校
blockbuster	[ˈblɒkbʌstə]	*n.*	大片(电影术语)
expect	[ɪkˈspekt]	*vt.*	期望;指望;认为;预料
suit	[suːt]	*vt.*	使适合;使适应
term paper			学期论文
what about doing sth.			做……怎么样
plan on			打算,计划
a war movie			一部战争片
promise to do sth.			承诺做某事
Chinese opera			中国戏剧

Practice

1. Finish the following dialogue according to the Chinese.

M: ________________ have dinner with me tonight? (今晚你愿意和我一起吃晚餐吗?)

W: Oh, ________________! (噢,听起来真不错!)

M: I'll pick you up at … say, 7:30?

W: ________________ (那很适合我们了。)

M: See you tonight then.

W: ________________. (好的。谢谢你的邀请。)

2. Finish the following dialogue according to the Chinese.

Chris 邀请 Liu 在星期六晚上到他家吃饭,Liu 欣然接受。

Chris: Hi, Liu! How are you?

Liu: Fine, thanks. And you?

Chris: Not bad. Liu, I wonder if ________________.

Liu: Yeah, thanks a lot. That would be great!

Chris: ________________?

Liu: Sure, Saturday evening would be fine. ________________?

Chris: Let's meet at six o'clock. Is that okay?

Liu: Great!

Chris: ________________?

Liu: Yeah. No problem. Thanks a lot. I really look forward to that.

◈ Culture Corner

（一）中西方文化在邀请上的差异

中国人邀请客人会准备一大桌子的菜，并在就餐过程中劝说客人多吃点，吃完之后，若有剩菜，就表明主人盛情款待了。而西方人不劝吃，而且就餐完毕后，盘子最好是空的。

在中国，人们往往会请客人在自己家里吃饭，要是在外就餐时，也会抢着买单。而在西方，外出就餐时，人们一般都实行 AA 制，各付各的账。

中国人经常会对别人说："哪天我请你吃饭啊。"这话听起来虽然很热情，但这样的邀请可能只是客套而已。而西方人的邀请一般比较慎重，他们一般不会随便邀请别人到家里做客，也不会轻易许诺邀请。

如果你不想在邀请这一环节上失礼，就要注意以下几个方面：

- 邀请重要人物最好单独宴请，这会让对方感到被重视、被尊重。如果邀请多人，则要权衡你打算邀请的客人彼此之间的关系，尽量邀请趣味相投的客人。如果需要的话，还可以邀请对方的配偶一道出席宴会，以体现对客人的尊重。

- 宴请的日期和时间要根据客人的具体情况来确定。一般要避开对方工作最为繁忙或是有重要活动的日子和时间段。可以事先给对方去电话，简单询问一下对方的时间安排和活动日程，并将自己确定的大概时间告知对方，双方共同商定最后的日期和时间，这既显得礼仪周全，又能保证宴会如期举行。

- 宴请的人选、时间确定之后，主方就应分发请柬。除了工作餐外，其他各种宴请都应发出请柬，以示对对方的尊重和重视。请柬应注明宴请人名、地点、时间等具体内容。如果是高规格宴请，请柬还应注明对出席者着装的要求。

- 请柬一般在宴请之前的一周内发出，太早客人容易遗忘，太晚则会使客人措手不及。请柬发出至举行的这段时间里，主方还可与邀请对象联系，以确定对方是否收到请柬、是否能准时出席。联系的最佳时间为宴请的前一两天。

（二）邀请中的"准时"

世界各地有关准时的指南：

对"准时"极为看重的国家：所有的北欧国家（斯堪的纳维亚诸国、德国、瑞士、比利时等）

对"准时"采取赞赏和期待态度的国家：加拿大、澳大利亚、英国、法国和美国。

对"准时"态度比较缓和的国家：欧洲南部（西班牙、意大利、希腊等国家），还有绝大多数地中海国家。

对"准时"持宽松态度的国家：绝大多数拉丁美洲国家和许多亚洲国家——在那里你尽管可以把手表抛在一边！

关于"准时"，不同国家、不同地区都会有不同的观念，所以无论你准备去哪里，你都应该事先了解一下当地人的时间观念。

Section 4 Making an Appointment

Warming-up

1. Match the words or phrases with the correct pictures.

A. interview	B. cheers	C. making a dating	D. cafe
E. red wine	F. on time	G. a bunch of flowers	H. Western restaurant

a. ________

b. ________

c. ________

d. ________

e. ________

f. ________

g. ________

h. ________

2. Work in pairs as follows.

A: Could I make an appointment with … tonight?

B: Yes. Why? /No, I'm afraid … can't make it, … have/has got an appointment with … else.

Sentence Patterns

约会常用语

I have an appointment with ... 我与……有个约会。

Are you going to be busy this evening? 今晚你忙吗?

Will it be convenient to see you on Monday? 星期一见面方便吗?

确定约会时间的常用套语

How about this afternoon? 今天下午怎么样?

Can you make it tomorrow? 明天你能行吗?

What time do you expect her? 你想让她几点来?

对请求约会及约会时间的回答

Yes. Why? Let's make it ... 好,就定在…… /No, I'm afraid I'm busy ... 不行,恐怕我很忙……

I'm afraid I can't make/manage it ... 我恐怕很忙……

I'm afraid it won't be very convenient. Could you make it some other time? 恐怕不方便,能另外约个时间吗?

I'll be looking forward to it/expecting you then. 我将期待那一天/到时我等你。

Communicating

Dialogue A

我一直想邀请 Miss Rose 一块吃顿饭,但她一直都不太方便:周四有讲座,周五和一位朋友有了约定,最后约定周六见面。

I: Hello, Miss Rose. Would you like to have a meal with us next week?

Miss Rose: Yes, I'd love to. When?

I: How about Thursday evening?

Miss Rose: I'm afraid I'll be busy preparing my lecture.

I: Are you free on Friday?

Miss Rose: Friday? Let me see. I've got an appointment with one of my friends.

I: So how about Saturday?

Miss Rose: Saturday sounds good. What time?

I: 6 p. m.

Miss Rose: 6 p. m. ? Fine, I'll be looking forward to it.

Dialogue B

Mike 打电话给 Doris 以确认他们之前安排的约见。

Doris: Hello!

Mike: Hello, is Doris available?

Doris: This is Doris. Who's that calling, please?

Mike: Hi, this is Mike. I'm calling to confirm your appointment.

Doris: Oh, thank you for calling. Actually, I can't make it that early.

Mike: What time do you expect?

Doris: Sorry, I'm afraid I can't manage it before 4. Would that be a better time?

Mike: That's OK. I think I am able to manage it at 4:15.

Doris: OK. Let's make it then.

Mike: I'll be expecting you then.

Vocabulary

prepare	[prɪˈpeə]	*vt.*	准备
appointment	[əˈpɔɪntm(ə)nt]	*n.*	任命;约定;任命的职位
convenient	[kənˈviːniənt]	*adj.*	方便的;适当的
available	[əˈveɪləbl]	*adj.*	空闲的;可得的;可利用的
confirm	[kənˈfɜːm]	*vt.*	确认;确定;证实;批准
manage	[ˈmænɪdʒ]	*vt.*	管理;经营;设法
expect	[ɪkˈspekt]	*vt.*	期望;指望;认为;预料
make it			赶上,达到,成功
look forward to			盼望,期待,期盼

Practice

1. Finish the following dialogue according to the Chinese.

Student: Excuse me, ______________________________(您知道张老师的办公室在哪里吗)?

Teacher: Are you looking for Zhang Bing? She's in Room 310 on the third floor.

Student: Yes. She told me to come by this morning.

Teacher: I'm sorry, but she's not in the office now. ____________________(你和她约好的吗)?

Student: An appointment?

Teacher: Yes. ______________________________(她想让你几点来)?

Student: She said I could come any time before noon.

Teacher: I see. But today she went out.

Student: That's too bad. I need to discuss these spoken English plans with her.

Teacher: ___________________________(明天能行吗)?

Student: Morning or afternoon?

Teacher: Morning.

Student: OK! ____________________________(我们就约在那时吧). Thank you.

Teacher: You are welcome.

2. *Choose the best answer from the box to complete the dialogue.*

A. What time would be good for you?
B. That's very nice of you.
C. It isn't very convenient for me then.
D. let's make it at 12:30.
E. Perhaps we can make it later.

A: I'm calling to see if you would like to have lunch with me tomorrow.

B: I'm sorry. ____________

A: Well, ____________

B: ____________ Thank you!

A: ____________

B: Well, ____________

A: Good, I'll see you there at 12:30.

Culture Corner

在国外如何约会

很多西方国家工作节奏都比较快,所以有事商谈需要预约,与某人预先约定叫 make an appointment with somebody 或者 fix an appointment with somebody; 守约是 keep one's appointment; 取消约会是 cancel an appointment; 失约是 break the appointment。

需要注意的是,在英语国家,人们都习惯于拟定好各自的日程安排。无论是出门旅游、看病,还是请客吃饭、参加娱乐活动、走亲访友,一般都要事先预约(appointment),否则会被认为是失礼的,有时还可能会碰钉子。比如,在英美国家,你若牙痛,去一家牙科诊所,但由于你未事先预约,医生可能会拒绝为你看病(当然若患了重病则是另外一回事)。又如你有事去拜访一个公司的经理,若事先没有预约,即使经理在,他也未必见你。约定的方式可以写信、打电话,也可亲自前往,除事务性的拜访必须有预约外,到普通朋友家(关系极为亲密的除外)做客也应通知一声,对普通朋友和熟人的拜访,预约时间也是非常必要的,因为人们通常不大欢迎不速之客(an unexpected guest),更不希望因此而使自己的计划受到影响。有了约定则要守时(punctuality),不守时也被认为是失礼的。若实在有特殊情况不能赴约,应事先通知对方推迟或取消约会。

美国人性格开朗,举止大方,乐于交际。他们平时晚睡晚起,但时间观念强;美国人会常说"随时来找我",有些邀约是相当诚恳的,但拜访前仍应事先电话联系,确定时间,以免自己的"随时"而给别人造成不便。若接到正式的邀约,请柬上倘印有「R. S. V. P.」,去与不去必须电话通知。大型活动请柬通常印有 Regrets only,此时只有不参加时才须通知。非正式私人邀请,可用电话或信函,明确告诉时间、地点。接到邀请,要回柬致谢;若没有赴约把握,就不要轻易应允;若不能应邀要说明理由,并致歉意。若临时不能赴约,务必电话通知。

在美国男女交往比较开放,约会、看电影、吃饭也是非常普遍的。男女双方均可主动邀约,通常男性较主动。可以 AA 制或一方请客。美国朋友倘若说:Let's go to get a beer 或 Want a cup of coffee? 可别误会他要请客,这种情形通常是各自付费。如果你想和某人或看个电影或一起吃个饭,以增进双方的友谊,共度一段愉悦的时光,尽可主动大方地去邀约。如果你不想赴对方约会,可以客气地说"NO"。

Section 5 Seeing Friends and Relatives

Warming-up

1. Match the words with the correct pictures.

A. uncle	B. classmates	C. aunt	D. grandpa
E. grandma	F. neighbour	G. cousin	H. brother

a. ________

b. ________

c. ________

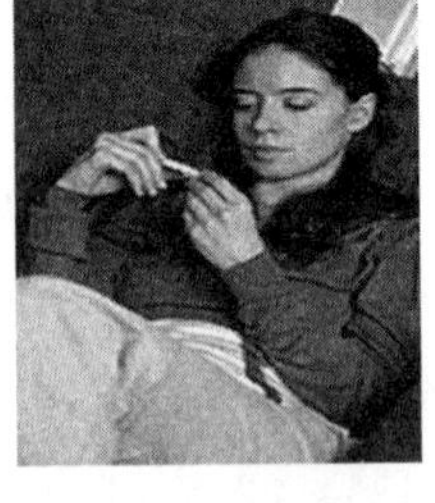

d. ________　　e. ________　　f. ________

g. ________　　h. ________

2. *Work in pairs as follows.*

A: How are you, my classmates/aunt/...

B: Nothing special.

Sentence Patterns

I	Friends and Relatives
How are you? Nice to see you. Where are you from? Are you married? Who is Silvia?	Nice to see you, too. All right. And you? I am from Yizheng, Jiangsu. No, I'm still alone. She is my cousin from America.

Communicating

Dialogue A

(*Lucy meets Mr. Wang.*)

Mr. Wang: Excuse me, are you Lucy?

Lucy: Oh, Mr. Wang!

Mr. Wang: Long time no see. How are you?

Lucy: Nothing special. So glad to meet you here!

Mr. Wang: Me too. It's been almost 5 years since we

last met.

Lucy: Yeah, how time flies! How are you these years?

Mr. Wang: Not much lately.

Dialogue B

A: Lily, this is Jack's cousin, David.

B: I'm very glad to meet you.

C: It's a pleasure to meet you.

B: How do you like London?

C: It's really different from what I expected.

B: Don't worry. You'll get used to it in no time.

Vocabulary

nothing special	没什么特别的
not much lately	还可以
different from	与……不同
get used to	习惯于
in no time	马上,立即

1. Finish the following dialogue according to the Chinese.

王兵向 Jack 介绍他的家人,Jack 说这是一个幸福的家庭,并询问王兵是哪国人,他的父母是否和他一起住在美国。王兵告诉 Jack 他是中国人,父母目前都住在中国。

Wang Bing: Jack, this is my mother, my father and my sister.

Jack: ____________, Wang Bing, Where ____________ you ____________?

Wang Bing: I'm from China.

Jack: ____________ your parents live here in the United States?

Wang Bing: No. Right now they ____________ China.

2. Finish the following dialogue according to the Chinese.

小李与玛丽约着一起去看电影,玛丽迟到了 10 分钟,因为路上正是交通高峰期,出了一点事情。他们匆忙赶向电影院,电影已经开始 5 分钟了。

A: Hi, Mary. You are behind for ____________.

B: I'm sorry. It's just ____________. Something came up on the way. The road was closed.

A: It's understandable. ____________. The film has already been on for five minutes.

B: ____________.

Culture Corner

（一）社交场合用语

在一般的社交场合，问候语要恰当得体，正式与非正式用语应区别运用。

正式场合的典型对话是：

A：Good afternoon, Mr. Reed. It is good to see you.

B：Thank you. It is nice to see you too. How are things going?

A：Just fine, thanks.

非正式场合中的对话：

A：Hi, Peter! How is it going?

B：Great! What's new with you?

A：Oh, not too much. You know, the same old thing.

（二）寒暄禁忌

两人交谈时，声音大小以对方听清为宜，不要在街上相距很远时高声交谈，也不要在大厅里、旅馆走廊里远距离打招呼、问候，而应在双方走近后才问候致意。

应避开疾病、死亡、灾祸以及其他不愉快的话题。此外，不要怨天尤人。可以交谈的话题包括天气、工作情况、住房情况、兴趣和爱好等。

切忌询问妇女年龄以及婚姻状况。西方女性对年龄和婚姻十分敏感，认为这些是个人隐私，他人不得干涉。切忌询问对方工资收入、财产状况、个人履历、服饰价格等私人问题。

在正式的场合中初次见面，双方握手会说 How do you do? 或 Pleased to meet you。非正式的场合中，年轻人见面寒暄 What's up? 后一般会说 Give me five（来握个手），然后两掌相击用力一握。

run into/come into/bump into 都表示"碰巧遇到"。非常熟悉的朋友偶遇后，还可以非常随意地说 Where have you been fooling around?（最近到哪里鬼混去了？）talk over coffee 边喝咖啡边聊天。over 相当于 while，如 sip over reading 一边读书一边喝茶；discuss over dinner 一边吃饭一边讨论。

英语中对亲戚的称呼跟中文是有区别的。双方的直系亲属（immediate family）都成了对方的姻亲 in-laws，比如 father-in-law，mother-in-law，sister-in-law，brother-in-law 等，英语对于亲属的称谓比中文要简单，西方人似乎不太在乎这位亲戚是父亲这边的（on the father's side），还是母亲那边的（on the mother's side），一视同仁，一个称呼，更有意思的是对远亲的称呼，cousin 一词不分男女，概括了所有堂兄弟和堂姐妹或者表兄弟和表姐妹。

表示职衔的称谓：assistant general manager 副总经理，auditor 审计员，president 大学校长，dean of school/college 学院院长，director of department 系主任，doctoral supervisor 博士生导师，visiting professor 客座教授，attending doctor 主治医师，editor-in-chief 总编。

表达同学关系的句子：We went to the same school（我们是校友）；We went to school together（我们是同级同学）；You are two years my senior /junior（你比我高/低两届）；She is my junior（她是我师妹）；He is my senior（他是我师兄）；alumnus 男校友，alumna 女校友；freshman 大学新生，sophomore 大二学生，junior 大三学生，senior 大四学生，undergraduate 在校生，postgraduate 研究生。

Module 3

Hotel California

Hotel California

On a dark desert highway, cool wind in my hair 在漆黑荒凉的高速公路上，凉风吹散了我的头发

Warm smell of colitas, rising up through the air 大麻温热的气息，在空中袅袅上升

Up ahead in the distance, I saw a shimmering light 抬头极目远方，看见微微闪烁的灯光

My head grew heavy and my sight grew dim 我的头脑变得沉重，我的视线越发模糊

I had to stop for the night 必须停下来了，寻找过夜的地方

There she stood in the doorway 她就站在门廊

I heard the mission bell 布道的钟声在我耳边回响

And I was thinking to myself, "This could be Heaven or this could be Hell" 我心中暗念，"还不知道这里是地狱还是天堂"

Then she lit up a candle and she showed me the way 这时她点起一根蜡烛，给我前面引路

There were voices down the corridor 走廊深处一阵阵歌声回荡

I thought I heard them say ... 我想我听见他们在唱……

"Welcome to the Hotel California" "欢迎来到加州旅馆"

Such a lovely place, such a lovely face 多么可爱的地方，多么可爱的脸庞

Section 1 Festivals

Warming-up

1. Look at the pictures below and work in pairs.

a. What do you know about the festivals in the pictures?

b. What can you often do in these festivals?

3. Can you tell any other festival both at home and abroad?

Sentence Patterns

Wishes & Congratulations	Responses
Happy New Year to you!	Thank you. And the same to you.
Merry Christmas to you!	I wish you the same.
Best wishes for …	Thank you.
All the best!	It's very kind of you to say so.
I wish you …	Thank you. Sure I'll do.
I hope that …	
May you succeed!	
Congratulations to you (on …)!	

(Continued)

Wishes & Congratulations	Responses
Happy birthday to you! Send my regards/wishes to your ..., please. Please remember me to your ... Have a good trip!	

Communicating

Dialogue

(*Tom meets his Chinese friend Wei Fang in the street just after Christmas.*)

Wei Fang: Merry Christmas, Tom!

Tom: Thanks, Wei Fang! And the same to you!

Wei Fang: Did you have a good time on Christmas Eve?

Tom: Yes, of course.

Wei Fang: How did you spend your Christmas Eve?

Tom: Dad brought home a big Christmas tree and my brother, my cousin and I decorated it with a lot of bells, toys and many other decorations.

Wei Fang: Your cousin was also at your home?

Tom: And my grandparents, my uncle, my aunt ...

Wei Fang: So many people! How interesting!

Tom: Mum prepared many delicious dishes, different kinds of snacks and drinks. We had a big dinner. And we children got many gifts, too.

Wei Fang: Sounds great! I wish you good health and success in the coming year.

Tom: The same to you. Please give my best wishes to your parents. I wish them the best of health.

Wei Fang: Thank you. Sure I'll do.

Tom: Not at all. By the way, how are you going to spend the holidays?

Wei Fang: I'd like a trip to New York.

Tom: Good idea. Have a good trip!

Wei Fang: Thank you.

Vocabulary

cousin	[ˈkʌzn]	*n.*	堂(表)兄弟(姊妹)
decorate	[ˈdekəreɪt]	*vt.*	装饰
decoration	[dekəˈreɪʃən]	*n.*	装饰,装饰品
snack	[snæk]	*n.*	小吃,零食
Merry Christmas!			圣诞节快乐!
on Christmas Eve			在平安夜
delicious dishes			美味佳肴
have a big dinner			吃一顿大餐
the coming year			来年
give best wishes to sb.			诚挚祝愿某人
have a good time			玩得痛快,过得愉快
decorate ... with ...			用……装饰……
different kinds of			各种各样的
have a good trip			旅途愉快

Practice

1. Finish the following dialogue according to the Chinese.

提示:Tony 和 Jenny 正在谈论即将到来的感恩节。Jenny 感叹时间过得真快,Tony 邀请她参加感恩节的庆祝宴会,Jenny 接受了邀请,并询问感恩节的由来。Tony 告诉她主要是人们向上帝表达谢意,主要食物有烤火鸡和南瓜饼。

Tony: Thanksgiving Day is round the corner.

Jenny: Is it? It's the last Thursday in November, right?

Tony: Yes!

Jenny: ____________!

Tony: I am thinking a ____________. I'd like to ____________.

Jenny: Great! Is there a special story on the holiday?

Tony: Yes! The early settlers had a good harvest. They thought they must ____________.

Jenny: Oh, I see! And what ____________?

Tony: We are going to prepare a big feast.

2. Make up the rest of the dialogue according to the Chinese above.

Culture Corner

美国的节日

在美国，有很多重要的节日。按时间顺序先后有：

1. 新年(New Year's Day)

1月1日美国人过新年，但最热闹的是新年前一天晚上。夜晚，人们聚集在教堂、街头或广场上，唱诗、祈祷、祝福、忏悔，并一同迎候那除旧迎新的一瞬间。午夜12点整，全国教堂钟声齐鸣，乐队高奏有名的怀旧歌曲《友谊地久天长》(Auld Lang Syne)。在音乐声中，激动的人们拥抱在一起，甚至素不相识的人也可以互相亲吻。人们就这样怀着对新生活的向往共同迎接新的一年。

虽然元旦并不是最热闹的一天，但仍有不少州举行极富地方色彩的庆祝活动。纽约市新年前夕，数万人聚集在时代广场看"大苹果"缓缓从空中落下，也是极有名的庆祝活动。

2. 情人节(Valentine's Day)

每年的2月14日，是3世纪殉教的圣徒圣瓦伦丁逝世纪念日。情人们在这一天互赠礼物，故又称 the Lovers' Day。

3. 复活节 (Easter)

复活节是基督教纪念基督 (Jesus Christ)复活的一个宗教节日，为美国的联邦假日。每年春分过去，第一次月圆后的第一个星期日就是复活节，约在3月7日左右。如果月圆那天正好是星期日，复活节将延迟一周举行。彩蛋(easter eggs)和兔子是复活节的象征。复活节的传统食品主要有羊肉和火腿。

4. 愚人节(April Fool's Day)

愚人节是从19世纪开始在西方兴起的民间节日，并未被任何国家认定为法定节日。每年4月1日这天，人们以各种方式互相欺骗和捉弄，往往在玩笑的最后才揭穿并宣告捉弄对象为"愚人"(April fool)。玩笑并无恶意，但个别玩笑由于开得过大会引起不必要的麻烦。

需要注意的是愚人节这天玩笑只能开到中午12点之前，这是约定俗成的严格规定，过了点还开玩笑的人会自找没趣。

5．母亲节（Mother's Day）

母亲节是一个感恩母亲的节日。母亲节的传统起源于古希腊。古希腊人向希腊众神之母瑞亚致敬。到古罗马时，这些活动的规模变得更大，庆祝盛况往往持续达三天之久。当然，古时人们对女神的崇拜只不过是一种迷信，它同今天人们对母性的尊敬是大不相同的。而现代的母亲节起源于美国，是每年5月的第二个星期日。政府部门和各家门口悬挂国旗，表示对母亲的尊敬。在家里，儿女们和父亲给母亲买些礼物或做些家务。

6．父亲节（Father's Day）

每年6月份的第3个星期天是父亲节。在家里，儿女们和母亲给父亲买些礼物表示对父亲的尊敬。

在父亲节这天，人们选择特定的鲜花来表示对父亲的敬意。佩戴红玫瑰向健在的父亲们表示爱戴，佩戴白玫瑰对故去的父亲表示悼念。父亲节在全美国作为节日确定下来，比母亲节经历的时间要长一些。因为建立父亲节的想法很得人心，所以商人看到了商机。他们不仅鼓励做儿女的给父亲寄贺卡，而且鼓动他们买领带、袜子之类的小礼品送给父亲，以表达对父亲的敬重。

7．万圣节（Halloween）

万圣节是西方的传统节日，时间为10月1日。万圣节前夜，孩子们装扮成妖魔鬼怪，手提“杰克灯”，跑到邻居家门前，高声喊着 Trick or treat，不给糖果的邻居就会遭到小孩的恶作剧，学校通常也有庆祝万圣节的化妆晚会。

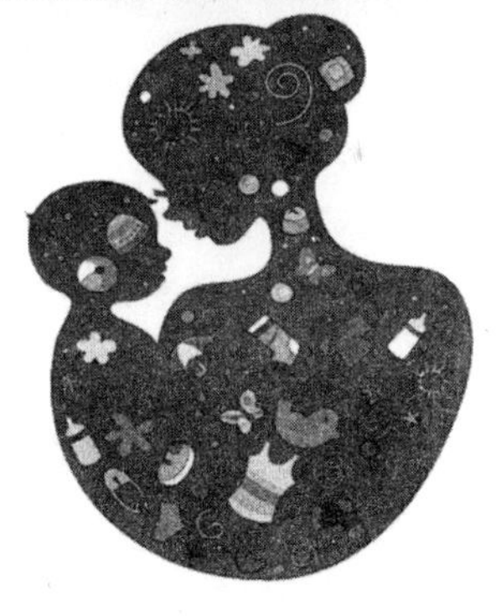

8．感恩节（Thanksgiving Day）

11月的最后一个星期四是感恩节，是美国人合家欢聚的节日，因此美国人提起感恩节总是倍感亲切。人们还要按习俗前往教堂做感恩祈祷。火鸡是家人团聚吃感恩节大餐的传统主菜。除此之外，还有红莓子果酱、甜山芋、玉蜀黍、南瓜饼及各种蔬菜和水果等。

9．圣诞节（Christmas）

12月25日圣诞节，纪念耶稣诞辰，是美国最大最热闹的节日。圣诞节的庆祝活动是从12月24日夜间开始，半夜时分达到最高潮。这一夜就被称为圣诞夜。人们有的聚在酒馆、舞厅、俱乐部中盛情欢乐；有的全家共进丰盛的晚餐，然后围坐在熊熊燃烧的火炉旁，共叙天伦之乐；虔诚的信徒们则在灯火通明的教堂里，参加纪念耶稣诞生的午夜礼拜。这是个一年一度大家交换礼物、卡片、叙旧问好的时节。到处可见装饰的琳琅满目的圣诞树，商店里挤满了买礼物的人，全国沉浸在一片温馨喜气的气氛中。

Section 2 Travelling

Warming-up

1. Match the places of interest with the correct pictures.

A. the Great Wall	B. the Eiffel Tower	C. Sun Moon Lake
D. Mount Huangshan	E. Terra-Cotta Warriors	F. the Temple of Heaven

a. ____________

b. ____________

c. ____________

d. ____________

e. ____________

f. ____________

2. Work in pairs as follows.

A: Where do you plan to spend your vacation?

B: I plan to spend my vacation in …

Sentence Patterns

A	B
Where do you plan to spend your vacation?	I plan to spend my vacation in …
Could you tell me where we'll visit on this tour?	Sure. We'll visit … and so on.
How long is this tour?	It's a full hour tour.
How can I travel there?	You may travel there by …
I hope you'll enjoy your trip.	Thank you!

Communicating

Dialogue A

(*Summer vacation is coming. Li Mei plans to go on a vacation next month. She asks Zhou Jun what she should do if she wants to go abroad.*)

Li Mei: Hello, Zhou Jun. I plan to spend my summer vacation abroad next month.

Zhou Jun: That sounds great! Where do you want to go?

Li Mei: I want to go to Sydney next month.

Zhou Jun: Well, if so, you'd better start getting ready for it now.

Li Mei: I know you have a lot of experience. What should I do?

Zhou Jun: Well, the applications for a passport and visa are the most important.

Li Mei: I see. Thank you! I'll prepare for it in the following days.

Zhou Jun: I hope you'll enjoy your trip!

Dialogue B

(*Li Mei is going to spend her summer vacation in Sydney next month. She is asking her friend Mary for suggestions.*)

Li Mei: Hello, Mary! I'm going to Sydney next month. I heard that it is your hometown.

Mary: Yes, it is. What are you planning to do during the trip?

Li Mei: First I will visit the Sydney Opera House. I think it is very beautiful.

Mary: That's true. It's also a wonderful place to enjoy a concert!

Li Mei: Great! Are there any other interesting places?

Mary: Why not go to the Australian Reptile Park? You can see many strange-looking animals.

Li Mei: Oh, I love koalas because they are so cute. I will surely go there.

Mary: There are also some other interesting places. And I'd like to be your guide when you come.

Li Mei: It's very kind of you to do so!

Mary: It's my pleasure.

Vocabulary

vacation	[vəˈkeɪʃn]	*n.*	假期
Sydney	[ˈsɪdnɪ]	*n.*	悉尼(澳大利亚最大的城市)
application	[ˌæplɪˈkeɪʃn]	*n.*	申请
passport	[ˈpɑːspɔːt]	*n.*	护照
visa	[ˈviːzə]	*n.*	签证
Australia	[ɒˈstreɪlɪə]	*n.*	澳大利亚
koala	[kəʊˈɑːlə]	*n.*	树袋熊,考拉
cute	[kjuːt]	*adj.*	可爱的,漂亮的
guide	[gaɪd]	*n.*	向导;导游
go abroad			去国外,出国
get ready			准备好
Sydney Opera House			悉尼歌剧院
Australian Reptile Park			澳大利亚爬行动物公园

Practice

1. Choose the best answer from the box to complete the dialogue.

A. Yes, it is all right.	B. Would you please fill in this form?
C. it is very cheap.	D. Which hotel do you want to put up?
E. Where do you want to go?	

A: Good morning! What can I do for you?

B: We'd like to make a trip for a weekend holiday.

A: There are many travel paths. ____________

B: We'd like to choose Jinggang Mountains.

A: It's really worth visiting. ____________

B: We're not sure. Which hotel do you think is comfortable?

A: The Holiday Home is very good. What's more important, ____________

B: We don't want to live in an expensive hotel.

A: ____________

B: OK. I'll ask my brother to fill in this form. By the way, is it all right if we pay by credit card?

A: ____________ Enjoy your weekend!

B: Thank you.

2. Finish the following dialogue according to the Chinese.

提示:暑假即将来临,徐慧和周伟正在讨论暑假去哪玩。周伟说他打算下周一和家人坐飞机去海南玩;徐慧说她非常想念祖父母,打算回乡去看望他们。他们互相祝愿彼此假期愉快。

Xu Hui: Hi, Zhou Wei. Where are you going to spend your summer holiday this year?

Zhou Wei: ________________.

Xu Hui: How are you going to get there?

Zhou Wei: We're going to get there by plane.

Xu Hui: ________________?

Zhou Wei: The next Monday.

Xu Hui: ________________.

Zhou Wei: Thanks. What about you?

Xu Hui: You know I'm from the country. ________________. I miss them very much.

Zhou Wei: ________________. I think you must have a good time in your hometown.

Culture Corner

出境旅游禁忌一览

一、东南亚篇

1. 日本

在日本,不管任何原因,都不能把筷子插入饭碗里离开,因为这是不祥的征兆。因为饭碗里直立的筷子会让日本人想起墓碑。

2. 印度

去印度旅游,吃饭和接拿东西,只能用右手,绝对不能用左手。因为这些国家的人一般在洗澡、上厕所时用到左手,左手是不洁净的,所以用左手接拿食品是对主人最大的不礼貌。

3. 泰国

绝不可骑在佛像上拍照,在东南亚的佛教国家,旅客如果对寺庙、佛像、和尚等做出轻率的行动,被视为"罪恶滔天”。有些不明利害的观光客，曾经由于跨坐在佛像上拍纪念照而被处以刑罚。另外，在泰国还有个规定，凌晨 2 时以后不准买酒，否则会被警察处以罚款。

4. 印尼

印尼等地的人们不希望别人摸自己身上的任何一部分，相对的。他们也不喜欢去摸别人。他们认为头部是人体最高的部分，也是人体中最神圣无比的部分，尤其是孩子的头，被视为神明停留之处。

5. 柬埔寨

在柬埔寨，如果你吃光盘子内所有的食物，表明主人没有招待好你，因为你没有吃饱还想要。

6. 新加坡

新加坡政府致力于保持清洁。乱丢垃圾初犯处以罚金一千元；累犯处以罚金两千元，依最新修订之惩治乱丢垃圾条例，新加坡全面禁售、禁食口香糖，口香糖为最难清除之垃圾之一。

二、欧美篇

1. 慎用“I am sorry”

在美国、英国，I am sorry 跟 Excuse me 所表达的意义截然不同。Excuse me（抱歉）是指无关紧要、轻描淡写的致歉语，使用 I am sorry 意义就相当深刻了，应慎用 I am sorry。

2. 翻书时不舔指头

翻阅书籍或数钞票的时候，很多人都有舔指头的习惯。这种动作，在欧美人士看来，既庸俗又不卫生。

3. 从坐着的人面前走过时要低头弯腰

在狭窄的场所，非别人面前走过不可的时候，要低身而过。在欧洲，你必须面对那个人低头弯身而过。在美国则恰恰相反，你必须背对着那个人低头弯身而过。

4. 进餐必须喝酒

到了葡萄牙，进餐时非得喝酒不可。要是搬出理由不喝，他们就认为你瞧不起他们。在葡萄牙，酒比水还便宜，酒精的含量也不高，因此进餐时同时喝些酒，绝不至于醉酒。

5. 不能送康乃馨

在法国，康乃馨被视为不祥的花朵。法国人什么都可以送，就是不能送康乃馨。

6. 立三脚架拍照

在希腊，拍照的时候绝不能大摇大摆地立三脚架来大拍特拍。这个国家有个规定：立三脚架的拍摄，必须获得官方的允许。他们认为，使用三脚架拍摄的人，是职业摄影家。

7. 忌讳 13

在德国，忌讳 13。要是 13 日碰巧又是个星期五，人们会特别小心谨慎。此外，德国人祝贺生日的习惯也不同于中国人。

8. V 手势

在大不列颠做 V 手势的时候掌心不要向内，因为这被认为是挑衅。据说 2 个手指的致意起源于英法百年战争。法国扬言要砍掉所有英国人射箭的手指头，结果最后英国大胜，因此摆出手指来炫耀自己是完好无损的。

9. 不能碰杯

匈牙利人敬酒的时候不会碰杯，因为奥地利人曾经在杀害 13 个匈牙利人后碰杯庆祝。之后的 150 年之内，没有任何一个匈牙利人在敬酒的时候碰杯。现在虽然过去很长时间了，但是这个传统还一直保留。

10. 忌短裤和无袖上衣

如果你打算在天气炎热的时候去意大利的教堂，出发的时候不要仅仅穿着短裤和无袖上衣。去意大利天主教大教堂的游客，无论是男士还是女士，都不允许只穿短裤和无袖上衣。在教堂门口会有警卫或教民检查，所以在出发的时候记得带上一件长袖衫或其他套头衫。

三、 非洲篇

1. 打招呼忌用左手

非洲流行的打招呼方式——举起右手、手掌向着对方，目的是表示“我的手并没有握石头”，它是友好的象征。

2. Negro 和 Black 是禁句

非洲人对 Negro、Black 二词不但有抗拒心理，而且不承认它的含义。称呼非洲人，最好照他们的国籍来称呼。

3. 用力握手是善意的表示

在非洲，握手时如果握得有气无力，被称为“礼貌不周”。他们认为，用力的程度跟对方好意的程度是成正比的。

4. 忌讳照相

非洲人普遍认为相机对准某物，某物的“精气”就给吸收殆尽。观光客如想拍摄，最好向对方先打个招呼，以免挨揍。

5. 不放盐

在埃及旅行的时候，不要在你的碗里加盐，因为这被看作对厨师的侮辱。

Section 3 Asking the Way and Giving Directions

Warming-up

1. Look at the pictures below and work in pairs.

a. Have you ever noticed the following traffic signs in the street?

b. What's the meaning of the traffic signs?

2. Can you tell me any other traffic sign in the street?

Sentence Patterns

Asking the Way	Giving Directions
Excuse me. Can you tell me the way to … Which is the way to … Where is the nearest … Could/Would you please tell me how to get to … I wonder if you could tell me how to get to … Am I going to … in the right direction? Can you help me out? I'm trying to find …	Turn left at the first crossing. Turn right at the second traffic light. Go down/along this road, and then you'll find … on your left/right. Just go straight until you reach … Take bus No. …, and get off at … It's quite far from here. You'd better take a taxi. I'm sorry. I'm new around, too.

◈ Communicating

Dialogue

(*It's the first day after Mr. Smith's arrival in Shanghai. He has lost his way. He asks Wang Lan the way to his hotel.*)

Mr. Smith: Excuse me. Will you please do me a favour?

Wang Lan: With pleasure. What is it?

Mr. Smith: I have lost my way. Could you tell me how to get to my hotel, the Holiday Inn?

Wang Lan: Oh, sorry, I'm a stranger here.

Mr. Smith: Well, thank you anyway.

Wang Lan: Why not ask the policeman over there? He's sure to know the way.

Mr. Smith: Oh, thank you!

(*A moment later*)

Mr. Smith: Excuse me, would you please tell me the way to the Holiday Inn?

Policeman: The Holiday Inn? Oh, just go straight until you reach the crossroad, then turn right and walk on until you see a post office. Your hotel is just next to it. You can't miss it.

Mr. Smith: And how far is it from here?

Policeman: Not too far, about a twenty-minute walk.

Mr. Smith: Can I take a bus there?

Policeman: I'm afraid there is no bus that goes in that direction. Actually, you can take the subway and get off at Park Street.

Mr. Smith: I see, but I'd rather walk. And I can enjoy the scenery along the way.

Policeman: That's a good idea!

Mr. Smith: Thank you very much. Goodbye!

Policeman: You are welcome!

Vocabulary

favour	[ˈfeɪvə]	*n.*	帮忙;支持,赞成
pleasure	[ˈpleʒə]	*n.*	愉快,乐趣;娱乐,消遣
stranger	[ˈstreɪndʒə]	*n.*	陌生人,外地人
miss	[mɪs]	*vt.*	错过;想念
subway	[ˈsʌbweɪ]	*n.*	地铁
		vi.	乘地铁
scenery	[ˈsiːnərɪ]	*n.*	风景,景色;舞台布景
do sb. a favour			帮某人一个忙
lose one's way			迷路
turn right			向右转
get off			下车
go straight			一直往前走
a twenty-minute walk			步行20分钟
enjoy the scenery			欣赏风景
with pleasure			很乐意

Practice

1. Finish the following dialogue according to the Chinese.

提示:一位老人向一位学生打听希尔顿旅馆在哪儿,然后又问去火车站的路,学生一一回答,老人一再表示感谢。

Elderly man: Excuse me, young man, ____________ the Hilton Hotel?

Student: The Hilton Hotel? Let me see. Oh, yes, go straight down this road. It's at the corner.

Elderly man: At the corner? ____________? On the left or on the right?

Student: On the right. Turn round the corner and you'll find it.

Elderly man: Straight to the right corner and turn round it. ____________.

Student: You are welcome.

Elderly man: By the way, ____________ to the railway station?

Student: You have to take a bus. It's quite a long way from here.

2. Make up the rest of the dialogue according to the Chinese above.

Culture Corner

（一）国外问路技巧

在国外，人生地不熟，免不了要问路，问路并非一件难事，有的时候通过问路还能让你体会到不同国家的不同文化以及不同种族的不同性格。

如果你懂英语，在英语国家问路要比在非英语国家方便点，只是英语国家的人讲起英语来往往语速较快，所以对英语听力的要求就高一些。听不懂的时候千万不要不好意思，干脆就要求对方讲慢一点。

在非英语国家问路往往要困难一些，但在不同的国家问路也是各有各的方法。

譬如，在西班牙或意大利，问路的时候直接用罗马字母读出地名就行，对当地人来说，即使你的发音有些怪异，往往也听得懂，而在法国问路用同样的方法就会洋相百出了。明明看着是罗马字母，可法语的读音却自成一体，要想问路就要事先学会所去地方的法语读音。譬如，香榭丽舍大街，如果你不会用法语说，法国人是绝对搞不明白你要去哪里的。

日本问路还是有个小窍门的，日本的地图或路牌基本都用日式汉字和罗马字母同时标注，刚好是一个表音一个表意，问路的时候，只要把音读出来就可以。

在韩国问路，看路牌（首尔的地铁站以及街头的路牌基本都由韩语、英语和汉语三种文字标注）的时候，如果稍微留意一下地名下面的罗马字母，再试着读一读的话，你一定会有意想不到的收获。

其实在国外问路大可不必担心自己的英语能否被理解，只要你问路的时候抓住地名，哪怕你问路时使用的是中文，对方也能大概猜到你的意思。假设有一个英语不太好的老外在北京向你问路，他想去三里屯，可是他的英语不太好，中文也一窍不通，但是他问路的时候把要去的地名三里屯说得非常清晰，你应该会明白他要去的地方。在国外问路也是一个道理！

（二）问路注意事项

1. 关于问路的对象，在城市里尽可能选择警察、协管员；户外时有时可供选择的问路人不多，总体上感觉中年以上的人群更可靠。

2. 你的言行举止很重要，要让人有信任感。

3. 一定要尊重别人，先真诚地向别人问好，再说明你要去的地方。当你问完了，不管对方所言是不是对你有帮助，也请你说声谢谢，并向人道别。

4. 问路时最好能把要去的地方的建筑或地形特点说出来，有些人不知道街道名称，但是一些标志性建筑耳熟能详。如果你没去过那些地方，最好也问下那里有什么标志，大概多远。

5. 最好多问几个人，因为每个人对距离的理解和表达方式不同。

Section 4 Taking a Taxi

Warming-up

1. Match the words or phrases with the correct pictures.

A. tip	B. driving license	C. take a taxi	D. taxi stand
E. receipt	F. license plate	G. change	H. traffic ticket

a. ________________

b. ________________

c. ________________

d. ________________

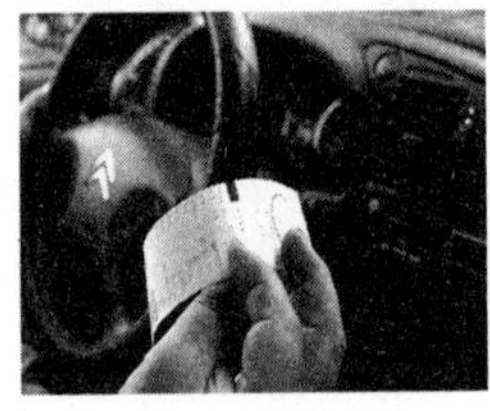

e. ________________

f. ________________

g. ________________

h. ________________

2. Work in pairs as follows.

A: Can you get us to the Yangzi Park?

B: With pleasure.

Sentence Patterns

Customer	Driver
What's the fare?	7 *yuan* within 3 kilometres, sir.
Hey, taxi!	Sure, my pleasure.
Excuse me, where can I take a taxi?	I feel terrible/bad.
Can you take me to Yizheng Technician College?	There's a taxi stand ahead.
Thanks a lot.	Have a good trip, sir.

Communicating

Dialogue A

Jack: Hello, take me to the Yizheng Bus Station, please. I want to catch the 11:10 bus.

Driver: I'll try my best. Step in, please.

Jack: How long will it take to get there?

Driver: Just 10 minutes, if the traffic is not heavy, 20 minutes at most.

Jack: Thank you. Please hurry.

...

Driver: Here you are. You are just in time.

Jack: Thank you. How much do I owe you?

Driver: 18 *yuan*, please.

Jack: Thank you so much indeed. That's 20 *yuan*. Please keep the change.

Dialogue B

Jane: Hey, could you take me to the Slender West Lake?

Driver: With pleasure. Welcome to Yangzhou.

Jane: Would you mind driving along travelling streets? I prefer the view.

Driver: All right. Yangzhou is a beautiful and peaceful city indeed.

Jane: Yes, you said it.

Driver: OK, we are here. That will be 15.8 *yuan*.

Jane: All right, here's the fare and the tip.

Driver: Thank you. Have a nice trip.

Vocabulary

traffic	[ˈtræfɪk]	*n.*	交通,运输
hurry	[ˈhʌrɪ]	*n.*	匆忙,急忙
		vi.	仓促(做某事),催促
owe	[əʊ]	*vt.*	应给予;应该把……归功于
fare	[feə]	*n.*	票价,费用
tip	[tɪp]	*n.*	小费;小建议,小窍门
		v.	给小费
the Yizheng Bus Station			仪征汽车站
the Slender West Lake			瘦西湖
Step in, please.			请上车
at most			最多
if the traffic is not heavy			如果交通不拥挤的话
Please keep the change.			不用找零了。
Would you mind doing …			你介意做……事情吗?
you said it			你说的对
Have a nice trip.			旅途愉快。

Practice

1. Finish the following dialogue according to the Chinese.

提示:Jack 正在打出租车去机场,他要赶 11 点的飞机,如果交通顺畅半小时能赶到。于是他们换道去了机场。

Jack: Hello, could you ____________ to the airport, please?

Driver: OK! Step in, please.

Jack: ____________ will it take to get there?

Driver: About thirty minutes if ____________.

Jack: I have to get there by 11 o'clock.

Driver: Do you mind making a detour?

Jack: Never mind. Thanks very much.

Driver: OK, ________________.

…

Jack: Thank you so much. ____________ should I owe you?

Driver: 26.5 *yuan*, please.

2. Choose the best sentence from the box to complete the dialogue.

A. How much do I owe you?	B. Keep the change, please.
C. Where do you want to go?	D. if there are no delays along the way

Tom: Taxi!

Driver: Get on, please. ____________

Tom: Thank you! Please hurry! Can I get to the Hongshan Park before 4?

Driver: All right. I think we'll get there ____________.

Tom: Thanks a lot.

Driver: Here we are.

Tom: Thank you. ____________

Driver: You owe me 19 dollars.

Tom: That's 20 dollars. ____________

Driver: Thank you, sir.

Culture Corner

各地打的

迪拜　平价便能乘豪车

来到迪拜这个遍地黄金和富豪的城市，打车也要有些"胆"，不是因为在迪拜打车不安全，而是在迪拜打车，分分钟可能拦到悍马、保时捷、宝马、奔驰等各种豪车的士。想想看，当这些动辄百万身价的豪车的士在你面前停下，司机热情地请你上车时，你是坐呢还是不坐呢？你会不会心里暗想着坐这样的豪车的士会不会贵得离谱呀，会不会宰客呀等问题？

可是，你这是在迪拜啊！迪拜最不缺的就是豪车，在大街上随随便便站着，都会发现各种高大上的车辆，奔驰、宝马的士其实并没有什么稀奇！至于大家担心的花销方面，听到价格之后一定会让你瞪大了眼睛，是的，迪拜的士就算是豪车的起步价也就3迪拉姆，即折合人民币6元，每千米价格为1.8迪拉姆，如果通过呼叫中心预订，起步费为6迪拉姆，而在晚上10点到第二天早上6点的起步价为3.5迪拉姆，预订费为7迪拉姆，折算起来都不算贵。所以下次在迪拜有需要打车时，记得拦下豪车坦然地坐进去哦！

华盛顿　特区

华盛顿出租车公司把市区划分为5个大区和27个小区，出租车在某一个区内行驶的收费是固定的，与行驶的里程无关，每个区里程计价的最低价是6美元；另有多人、低速、行李、高峰等附加费以及10%的小费，但市区资费19美元封顶。

注意，华盛顿的出租车只能在市区内行驶，不能离开特区，而从邻近的弗吉尼亚或者马里兰州搭乘出租车进入华盛顿则没有问题。

巴黎 收费多多不抵坐

在巴黎“打的”是件费钱的事，本身起步价和里程价就不便宜，还要加上各种额外的收费，名目繁多，可能连当地人都算不过来。比如，打车费包括起价费、按公里计行驶费、等候费或低速行驶费，另外还会分时间计价，比如从 7 点至 19 点为正常价，从 19 点到次日 7 点算夜间价，星期天和节日全天按夜间价计，还可能分行驶区间计价，即在市区和去郊区的价格不同。最要命的是，巴黎出租车还有附加费，并且名目五花八门，比如在火车站、机场或有特殊指示牌的地方乘车，需加付 0.7 欧元，有大型物件（如滑雪橇、自行车等），需加付0.9 欧元等，另外巴黎的出租车还会设置狗席，狗狗上座也是要收费的。

沙特 微笑等于不尊重

在沙特打车，一定要注意自己的表情，上了车不要以微笑表示友好，司机会认为这是种极大的不尊重，甚至是对自己的一种侮辱！虽然这种情况在这两年随着游客的增加有所改变，但在出租车上还是最好从头到尾板着面孔，不要说一句话。另外，在沙特打车并不是很正规，最好先讲好价钱和所要去的地方，很多地方因为路途远或没有回头客或其他原因司机是不愿意去的，在这种情况下，最好先咨询一下导游或酒店前台，即便贵一点，包车也好过在路边打车。

阿根廷 坐前座是丢脸事

阿根廷人打车不坐前座，原因是阿根廷人认为坐在司机旁边是件丢人的事，虽然这个习惯的根源并不是当地人有意歧视出租车司机，可能是因为觉得坐在后排更像顾客。

总体来说，在阿根廷布宜诺斯艾利斯这样的大城市里，打车是相对比较容易的，和国内一样，你可以在路上拦空车，正规的出租车是黄色的顶、黑色的车身，白天起步价是 9.1 比索，夜间计费从 22:00 到 6:00，起步价 10.9 比索。不过要注意，坐车时最好准备零钱，因为有些出租车司机会没有零钱找给你。

其实，在阿根廷境内还可以采用一种私车服务，即 Remise。这种车也有正规的牌照，但车子里面没有设置里程计价器，一般是由司机和乘客事先谈好一个到达某个目的地的价格，然后直接将客人送到目的地。这种车是需要电话预约的，沿街拦不到，价格相对比出租车贵，对于游客来说，还需要通过当地导游或是酒店帮忙，才能找到这样的车。

埃及 货比三家“腰斩”价

在埃及打车是不跳表的，很多出租车不装计价器，或是计价器只作为一个摆设。在埃及搭乘出租车，要注意先和司机谈好价格再上车。具体要说清楚要去哪里，再和司机谈车费，而一些司机会对游客漫天要价，最好货比三家，多问几个司机，也不用害怕砍价，从司机提出的价格“腰斩”一半开始谈是平常的事。

Section 5 Booking Airline Tickets

Warming-up

1. Match the the words or phrases with the correct pictures.

A. boarding pass	B. discount ticket	C. CAAC	D. economy class
E. book tickets	F. airport	G. stewardess	H. security

a. ________________

b. ________________

c. ________________

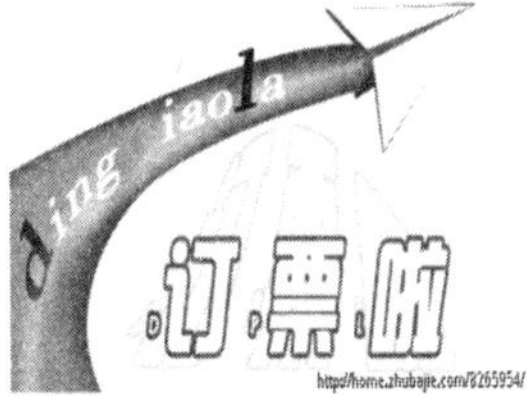

d. ________________

e. ________________

f. ________________

g. ________________

h. ________________

2. Work in pairs as follows.

A: Would you please reserve two seats to London for me?

B: Wait a moment, please. I'll check.

Sentence Patterns

Customer	Attendant
What's the fare to New York, the economy class?	Wait a moment, please. I'll check.
What time does it take off?	Have a nice trip.
Would you please reserve two seats to London for me?	OK. What flight would you like?
	9 a. m. , sir.
May I change my reservation?	That's 350 dollars altogether.
That's fine. I'll take it.	I'm sorry, sir. All the seats are reserved.

Communicating

Dialogue A

(*B is reserving a ticket to London on the telephone.*)

A: May I help you?

B: Yes, I'd like to reserve an economy class seat to London. Are there any seats for tomorrow?

A: I'm sorry, sir. All the seats are reserved.

B: Oh, I see. How about a Saturday flight?

A: Just a second. I'll check ... Yes, sir, we do have an available seat on CAAC Flight 901.

B: What time does it take off?

A: At 11 at noon, sir. And it gets to London at 2:30 p. m.

B: That's fine. I'll take it.

Dialogue B

A: I'd like to book two tickets to New York for this Thursday.

B: Just a moment, please. I'll check.

Yes, sir. We have two seats available on Flight 402 at 8:15 a. m. OK?

A: Will it be there by noon?

B: Sure. It gets to New York at 10:45.

A: That'll be fine.

B: All right. Will that be a one-way or round trip?

A: One-way, please.

B: That's 308 dollars altogether, sir.

A: Thank you very much.

B: Our pleasure, sir. Have a good trip!

Vocabulary

reserve	[rɪˈzɜːv]	*vt.*	预订
London		*n.*	伦敦
Saturday	[ˈsætədɪ]	*n.*	星期六
Thursday	[ˈθɜːzdɪ]	*n.*	星期四
flight	[flaɪt]	*n.*	飞行
New York			纽约
altogether	[ˌɔːltəˈgeðə]	*adv.*	完全地;总共
economy class			经济舱
CAAC Flight 901			中国民航901次航班
all right			好的
get to			到达
a round trip			一张往返票
Have a good trip!			祝你旅途愉快!

Practice

1. Finish the following dialogue according to the Chinese.

提示:Tom准备订一张本周飞往Boston(波士顿)的机票,票务员Lucy询问他是买经济舱还是头等舱,Tom订了头等舱,并问价格,Lucy说单程225美元,于是Tom订了单程头等舱。最后票务员留了Tom的个人信息及联系方式,以便及时联系他。

Lucy: Good morning. ________________?

Tom: Yes, I'd like to ________________ to Boston this week.

Lucy: OK. Just a moment, please. Let me check whether there are seats available.

Tom: Thank you.

Lucy: There are also some seats now, sir. You want to go ________________ or economy?

Tom: I prefer the first class. ________________?

Lucy: One way is $225.

Tom: OK. I will take the 9:30 Flight on Saturday.

Lucy: Right. ________________?

Tom：My name is Tom. You can reach me at 62478356.

2. Make up the rest of the dialogue according to the Chinese above.

Culture Corner

美国机场入境注意事项

一、入境检查手续

外籍人士进入美国，必须要持有一个有效的签证。无论是移民签证还是非移民签证，都是由美国驻海外领事馆签发的。外籍人士以非移民身份进入美国，除了一个有效的非移民签证外，还必须持有一本6个月以上有效期的护照，且护照有效期应至少为计划停留美国的时间外再加上6个月。

1. 入境表格(Entry Form)

在飞往美国的途中，空中小姐会分发旅客I-94出入境记录卡(Arrival/Departure Record Card)和海关申报单(6059B Customs Declaration Form)。在飞机着陆前，每位旅客必须按规定用英文填写好入境表格。如不懂英文，可向空姐询问或请她协助填写。

2. 出入境卡(I-94)

CBP (US Customs and Border Protection)宣布，从2013年4月底开始将I-94卡片部分电子化。乘坐商业航班进出境的外国旅客绝大多数情况下将无须填写I-94表格。美国海关可以从航空公司那里获取乘客的出入境信息，这样既提高了出入境效率，同时也节约了纸资源。

3. 海关申报单(Customs Declaration Form)

所有入境的旅客(All Persons)，无论是美国公民还是外籍人士，都必须填写。

若是一个家庭，只需填写一份。

4. 入境手续(Entry Procedures)

在飞机抵达美国机场后，旅客会由航空公司人员引导，进入入境检查大堂。旅客无论已到达最后目的地或还要转机去美国其他城市，都必须在第一个入境的美国口岸(First US Port-of-Entry)办理入境检查手续。

· 移民局(Immigration)核实入境者的入境身份与文件

· 农业部(Agriculture)检验有关食品与动植物

· 海关(Customs)检查所有进入美国的物品

5. 检查通道(Inspection Lanes)

在入境检查大堂，旅客应按照本人的入境身份(居民或非居民)，排入不同的通道，等候入境检查。

使用公民/居民(Citizen/Resident)标志通道入境之人士：

· 入境美国的美国公民(US Citizens)

· 返回美国的永久居民/绿卡外籍人士(Returning Resident Aliens)

· 持移民签证首次入境的新移民外籍人士(Aliens with Immigrant Visas)

使用非公民(Non-Citizens)或非居民(Non-Residents)标志通道入境之人士:

· 其他所有的外籍人士(All Other Aliens),包括持非移民签证(Non-immigrant Visa)者

6. 入境盖章(Entry Stamp)

入境外籍旅客应把护照、I-94 出入境卡、海关申报单及相应入境文件,按顺序夹入美国签证页,一并交给移民官接受检查和询问。通常移民官会在一分钟之内决定允许你入境与否。若允许你入境,在检查结束后,移民官会在护照页盖章。

持非移民签证者(Non-immigrant Visa Holder)

· 在申请人的 I-94 卡与护照上盖章并注明在美停留的期限

· 在申请人的护照上盖章并注明 I-551 移民身份临时证明及入境记录,包括其移民签证种类(Classification),及未收到正式绿卡前在美临时移民身份的有效期限(Expiration Date)

二、 领行李,缴报关单及验关

1) 根据走道上的指示走到 Terminal 领行李处,依电脑屏幕或告示找到自己班次的行李招领台。

2) 从转盘上取下自己的行李,小心核对行李号码,因为不少皮箱看起来一模一样。

3) 机场备有手推车。也可以找行李员 porter 代劳。

4) 国际机场很大,领行李时常容易找错转盘。有时航空公司也会疏忽。找不到行李别紧张,持登机证上的行李注册存根向航空公司查询,万一还是找不回来,则须填写报失单,并记下机场服务人员的姓名及电话,以备日后询问。

5) 排队验关时,不妨选最短一行排队受检。不要左顾右盼,犹豫不决,更不可看另一行通关迅速而临时换行,态度诚恳,有问必答,但不要多话,以免自找麻烦。

6) 检查行李时要递上证件,如海关要求开箱检查,立刻打开受检,不要迟疑。如果验关人员示意通过,也不要怀疑,立刻拿上行李离开。

7) 如果在行李中被发现有任何禁带物品,是要被当场没收的。

8) 随时注意自己行李证件,不可离身,以防被人乘机盗取。

9) 携带入境的金额超过一万美元,应主动向海关申报,并填报 4790 表。

三、 转机

如果你入境后要转机，你得估计好时间，尽早到要转换的航空公司机场柜台去报到，当然行李还是要重新 check in。如果机场大，为避免走冤枉路，不妨问一下人。将换机手续办妥。

转机旅客在购票时要注意航班之间的衔接时间，国内与国内航班衔接时间不得少于 2 小时，国内与国际航班衔接时间不得少于 3 小时。

转机旅客到达中转站机场后，可向机场地面服务人员提出，服务人员将会提供咨询和引导服务。

转机旅客可在中转柜台或续程航班的值机柜台办理乘机手续，如在上一航班办理了行李托运的，须把托运行李取出，再到续程航班的值机柜台办理。

国内航班中转旅客航班衔接时间在 8 小时以内的，转机时无须再购买机场建设费，但旅客须保存好上一航班的机票及机场建设费，以备检查。

Section 6 At the Hotel

Warming-up

1. Match the words or phrases with the correct pictures.

A. booking a room	B. single/double/standard room/suite	
C. room key	D. luggage/baggage	E. room service
F. wake-up service	G. laundry	H. bill

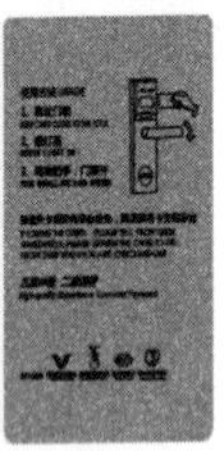

a. ________

b. ________

c. ________

d. ________

e. ________

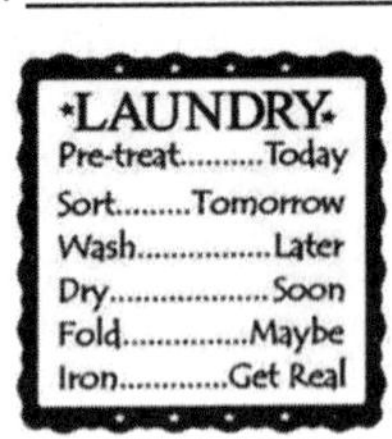

f. ________

g. ______________ h. ______________

2. *Work in pairs as follows.*

A: Good afternoon, sir. Welcome to Liming Hotel.

B: Thank you.

Sentence Patterns

Receptionist	Guest
Hello, this is Liming Hotel. Can I help you?	Yes, I'd like to book a standard room from October 1th to 7th.
Hello. I have a room reserved at the hotel.	You're in Room 888 on the third floor. Here's your key card.
May I help you with your luggage, madam?	Thank you.
Does your hotel provide room service?	Yes, we serve full meals. There will be a menu in your room.
The total charge comes to $186. Will you pay by the credit card?	No. Cash.

Communicating

Dialogue A

(*John is at Liming Hotel.*)

Receptionist: Good morning! Welcome to our hotel, sir. What can I do for you?

John: Glad to meet you. My secretary booked a double room here yesterday. Here's my passport.

Receptionist: It's Room 888. Please fill in the form.

John: OK. Will someone help me with my luggage?

Receptionist: Of course. Here's your key card. Wish you a good dream tonight.

John: Thank you.

Dialogue B

(*The next day*)

Receptionist: Good morning! What about last night?

John: I haven't recovered from the jet lag. Do you provide the room service?

Receptionist: Yes. There will be a menu in your room. The dinning room is on the first floor.

John: Thank you.

(*One week later*)

Receptionist: Hello!

John: Hi, I want to check out.

Receptionist: The bill comes to $896.

John: The credit card, please.

Receptionist: OK. Please sign your name here. Wish you a good journey.

John: Thank you.

Vocabulary

passport	[ˈpɑːspɔːt]	*n.*	护照,通行证
luggage	[ˈlʌɡɪdʒ]	*n.*	行李;皮箱
recover	[rɪˈkʌvə]	*vt.*	恢复
jet lag			时差感,飞行时差反应
menu	[ˈmenjuː]	*n.*	菜单;菜肴
book a room			订房间
key card			房卡
room service			客房服务
dinning room			餐厅,饭厅
check out			退房;结账
come to			共计

Practice

1. Finish the following dialogue according to the Chinese.

提示:John 想订房间,黎明大酒店的服务员告诉他有单人间、标准间。标准间 120 元一晚，单人间 100 元一晚。John 订了单人间。John 询问客房服务，服务员告诉他宾馆提供正餐，房间有菜单，餐厅在一楼。John 问干洗是否免费，服务员告诉他不免费。服务员问 John 是否需要叫醒服务，John 说需要，因为时差还没倒过来。一星期后，John 用信用卡结账离开，服务员祝他一路顺风。

Receptionist: Good morning, Liming Hotel. ________________?

John: Yes. ________________.

Receptionist: OK. We have single and standard rooms.

John: That's nice. ________________?

Receptionist: A standard room with double beds costs ￥120 and a single room ￥100.

John: ________________.

Receptionist: OK.

2. Make up the rest of the dialogue according to the Chinese above.

◈ Culture Corner

（一）入住宾馆

1. 外国人入驻中国的宾馆

在中国入住宾馆，需要出示本人的有效身份证件，如身份证等。外国人入住中国的宾馆，可以请中国人帮忙预订，也可以自己出示护照，直接登记入住。

2. 入住国外的宾馆

在国外不管下榻星级宾馆还是一般旅店，都要按规定办理入住手续。其一般程序为：(1)办理预订手续。客人可通过电话预订方式等，预订时要把自己的姓名、性别、国籍和护照号码等信息告知宾馆或旅店，并取得确认单。(2)到达宾馆前台，出示预订的确认单后，服务人员则会交给旅客一份登记表。登记表的内容和国内星级宾馆的表格内容基本一致，主要包括旅客姓名、性别、护照号码、信用卡种类及号码，以及拟住天数等。旅客按要求填写完毕后，要连同护照一起交回服务人员。服务人员检查确认并安排好房间后，即将房间钥匙和护照交给旅客。旅客拿到钥匙后即可到房间入住。(3)如事先未办理客房预订手续，也可直接到自己认为适合入住的宾馆前台询问有否有空余房间并办理登记入住手续。(4)进入房间后，行李员则随即将行李送到房间。旅客检查无差错后，应表示谢意并同时付给小费。

（二）宾馆的主要构成

前厅部

一般位于酒店一层大堂，为住客办理订房、入住登记、咨询以及行李存取等一系列服务。您在旅程中遇到的任何问题都可以向前台服务人员进行询问。此外，酒店前台还可以为您提供叫早、订车以及其他代办服务。

客房部

您旅程的舒适度与客房部提供的服务密不可分。主要表现在您入住房间的整洁卫生、用品齐全、设施完好等方面。此外，您对热水、洗衣、熨衣等方面的要求也由这一部门来为您完成。

餐饮部

多数酒店都拥有两至三家以上的餐厅以及咖啡厅、酒吧等，为您提供餐饮方面的服务。由于酒店讲究的是服务质量，所以它的价格也是比较昂贵的。

保安部

负责住店客人安全。如遇黑车宰客、强行兜售、倒汇换汇、偷盗等情况发生均可向前台及保安人员求助。

康乐部

可分以下几个部分：健身房、器械健身、球类健身、游泳、桑拿、按摩等。

娱乐：卡拉OK、舞厅、表演等。

美容美发：化妆、按摩美容、理发、染发等服务。

医疗服务

一般高星级酒店都设有医务室，但只为宾客治疗常见的小病、小伤，对严重的或判断不准的，将负责替客人联系就近的大医院进行救治。

Module 4

High School Never Ends

High School Never Ends

Four years you think for sure 确信四年熬完

That's all you've got to endure 一切就会过去

All the total dicks 所有的白痴

All the stuck up chicks 所有爱出风头的小妞

So superficial, so immature 都是那么做作和幼稚

Then when you graduate 终于毕业了

You take a look around and you say HEY WAIT 看看周围的一切

This is the same as where I just came from 怎么跟高中一模一样

I thought it was over 还以为都已结束

Aw that's just great 真是不爽

The whole damn world is just as obsessed 这疯狂的世界只在乎

With who's the best dressed and who's having sex 谁最会打扮，谁和谁相爱

Who's got the money, who gets the honeys 谁是大款，谁是万人迷

Who's kinda cute and who's just a mess 谁挺可爱，谁是垃圾

And you still don't have the right look 而你还是没有所谓"好看"的外表

And you don't have the right friends 还是没有交到所谓的挚友

Nothing changes but the faces, the names, and the trends 啥都没变，除了面孔、名字和流行元素

High school never ends 高中永远不会结束

Section 1 Life on Campus

Warming-up

1. Match the words or phrases with the correct pictures.

A. opening ceremony	B. office building	C. freshman	D. make a speech
E. teaching building	F. Yizheng Technician College		G. dormitory
H. training room			

a. ________________

b. ________________

c. ________________

d. ________________

e. ________________

f. ________________

g. ________________

h. ________________

2. Work in pairs as follows.

A: How do I address you? /May I have your name?

B: My name is … /I'm …

Sentence Patterns

Freshman	Classmate
How do I address you?	Nice to meet you. I'm ...
What's your major?	My major is .../I'm a ... major.
Do you major in ...	I major in ...
What year are you in?	I'm a freshman/sophomore/junior/senior.
Would you show me around the campus?	I'm glad to.
Have you got your work done for today?	Yeah, I have handed it in to the professor.
When is the test/final examination again?	It's ... /I'm not sure.

Communicating

Dialogue A

(*Li Lei is a freshman admitted by the Department of Electrical Engineering of Yizheng Technician College.*)

Li Lei: I am new here.

Schoolmate A: You are welcome.
How do I address you?

Li Lei: Nice to meet you. I'm Li Lei. May I have your name?

Schoolmate A: I'm Li Fei.
What year are you in?

Li Lei: I'm a freshman. And you?

Schoolmate A: I'm a sophomore.

Li Lei: What's your major?

Schoolmate A: I'm a Mechanical and Electrical Engineering major.

Li Lei: Well, I am in the Department of Electrical Engineering.

Dialogue B

(*Another day, Li Lei met another schoolmate, and talked with him.*)

Li Lei: Would you like to show me around our campus?

Schoolmate B: I'm glad to.

Li Lei: Is the campus large?

Schoolmate B: Yes. You can find a lot of buildings, such as the office building, the science building, the training building and so on.

Li Lei: What's that building on the right?

Schoolmate B: It's our main teaching building.

Li Lei: What's that over the training building?

Schoolmate B: It's the playground, the campus stadium and gymnasium.

Li Lei: How can I check what my advisor is?

Schoolmate B: Yeah, just check the information on Yizheng Technician College web page.

Li Lei: Could you tell me where the canteen on campus is?

Schoolmate B: Yeah, it's just down this walkway and to the left.

Li Lei: Many thanks. See you another day.

Schoolmate B: You are welcome! See you.

Vocabulary

admit	[ədˈmɪt]	*vt.*	录取;承认
address	[əˈdres]	*vt.*	称呼;演说;向……致辞
freshman	[ˈfreʃmən]	*n.*	大学一年级学生;新手,生手
major	[ˈmeɪdʒə]	*n.*	主修科目
campus	[ˈkæmpəs]	*n.*	(大学)校园;大学,大学生活
stadium	[ˈsteɪdiəm]	*n.*	体育场;露天大型运动场
gymnasium	[dʒɪmˈneɪziəm]	*n.*	体育馆;健身房
advisor	[ədˈvaɪzə]	*n.*	顾问;提供意见者
canteen	[kænˈtiːn]	*n.*	食堂,小卖部
Mechanical and Electrical Engineering			机电工程系
Department of Electrical Engineering			电气工程系
training building			实训楼
web page			网页

Practice

1. Finish the following dialogue according to the Chinese.

提示:报到后的一天,李磊在校园内又碰到了一位住在校内的大三校友,互相介绍后,询问了学校食堂、住宿和附近药店的情况。

Schoolmate: ____________?

Li Lei: I'm Li Lei.

Schoolmate: ____________?

Li Lei: I'm a freshman.

Schoolmate: ____________.

Li Lei: This is a large and beautiful campus, isn't it?

Schoolmate: Yes.

Li Lei: Do you live on or off campus?

Schoolmate: ____________.

Li Lei: ____________? I've got the flu.

Schoolmate: Yeah, it's just down this walkway and to the right.

Li Lei: Thanks a lot. See you.

Schoolmate: See you another day.

2. Choose the best answer from the box to complete the dialogue.

提示:李磊进入学院快半学期了,感触很多,和同学谈起了和室友的相处、作业以及为即将而来的期中考试做准备等情况。

A. When will we take the mid-term examination?
B. Take it easy.
C. I have handed it in to professor Zhang.
D. How do you get along with your roommates?
E. I don't think I'm ready for this class.

Classmate: ____________

Li Lei: Very well. Have you got your homework done for today?

Classmate: Yeah, ____________

Li Lei: I hope he goes over our homework.

Classmate: Me too. ____________

Li Lei: Next Wednesday. ____________ It seems so hard!

Classmate: Did you study for the test?

Li Lei: I'm afraid not.

Classmate: ____________ Try our best to prepare for it. OK?

Li Lei: No problem.

Culture Corner

(一) 美国课程和图书馆

美国的课程和中国的不太一样。美国的课程设置是学分制。也就是说,每个学生必须修够规定的学分,而且保证成绩在及格以上。无论本科还是研究生都按照这个制度去实施。只不过研究生的课程较少,但课程密度大,论文和阅读很多,尤其美国文科硕士很辛苦。本科课程较多,大概一学期要修5~6门课,但课程密度不是很大,一般只要保证期中和期末考试在及格以上就好。另外,美国按季度分为四个阶段,分别是春季学期、夏季学期、秋季学期、冬季学期。一般夏季学期的学费较贵,一些提前毕业的学生可以在夏季学期选几门课程,冬季学期情况类似。对于一般学生来说,主要是春季学期和秋季学期,因为很多学校招生也是按照这个制度来进行的,招生日期一过,就不再招收学生了。

国外正规的大学都有很完备的图书馆。在图书馆进行学术研究是很方便的。另外,图书馆也提供很多学习房间,有的甚至是24小时开放的。有的学生累了就在图书馆的沙发上睡会儿,醒了后继续学,这一般发生在期中和期末前后,那时图书馆爆满。很多大学图书馆之间都有合作,有的书在本校图书馆里找不到,学生就可以申请向其他图书馆借,一般只需几天的时间图书馆就能帮学生找来需要的书。

(二)世界著名大学校训(中英对照)

1. University of Oxford: The lord is my illumination.

牛津大学:上帝赐予我们知识。

2. University of Cambridge: Here light and sacred draughts.

剑桥大学:求知学习的理想之地。

3. University of Edinburgh: The learned can see twice.

爱丁堡大学:智者能看到表象,也能发现内涵。

4. Harvard University: Let Plato be your friend, and Aristotle, but more let your friend be truth.

哈佛大学:以柏拉图为友,以亚里士多德为友,更要以真理为友。

5. Yale University: Light and truth.

耶鲁大学:真理、光明。

6. Massachusetts Institute of Technology(MIT): Mind and hand.

麻省理工学院:理论与实践并重。

7. Columbia University: In the light shall we see light.

哥伦比亚大学:在上帝的启示下我们寻找知识。

8. Dartmouth College: A voice crying in the wilderness.

达特茅斯学院:广漠大地上(对知识)的呼唤。

9. United States Military Academy at West Point: Duty, Honor, Country.

西点军校:职责、荣誉、国家。

10. University of Michigan: Art,Science,Truth.

密歇根大学:艺术、科学、真理。

11. Toronto University: As a tree with the passage of time.

多伦多大学:像大树一样茁壮成长。

12. London University: Let everyone come to the university and merit the first prize.

伦敦大学:我们为至高荣誉齐聚于此。

13. University of Cape Town: Good hope.

开普敦大学:美好的希望。

14. Queen's University: Wisdom and knowledge shall be the stability of the times.

皇后大学:智慧和知识将是未来时代的稳定之基。

15. Hokkaido University: Boys, be ambitious!

北海道大学:孩子们,树立远大的理想和抱负吧!

16. University of Sydney: Although the stars may change, our mind remains the same.

悉尼大学:物换星移,心智相通。

17. Tsinghua University: Self-discipline and social commitment.

清华大学:自强不息,厚德载物。

Section 2 Sports and Fitness

Warming-up

1. Match the sports with the correct pictures.

A. playing football	B. playing baseball	C. going running	D. going cycling
E. playing badminton	F. doing taekwondo	G. playing basketball	H. doing yoga

a. ________________

b. ________________

c. ________________

d. ________________

e. ________________

f. ________________

g. 　　h. ______________

2. *Work in pairs as follows.*

A: What's your favorite sport?

B: My favorite sport is ...

Sentence Patterns

Partner A	Partner B
What kind of sport do you like?	I like jogging and going swimming.
What's your favourite sport?	My favourite sport is playing football.
You look so slim. How do you keep fit?	I often work out in the health club.
How often do you take exercise?	Once/Twice/Three times a week.
How about doing yoga at the gym?	That's great. /Good idea!
I need to get some more exercise.	You can go with me next time.

Communicating

Dialogue A

(*Rose meets Lucy by the sea, and Lucy is taking exercise.*)

Rose: Hello! Good morning! What are you doing?

Lucy: Hi! I am doing yoga.

Rose: Do you often work out by the sea?

Lucy: Yes, quite a bit. How about you?

Rose: Hmmm ... I like swimming.

Lucy: How often do you go swimming every week?

Rose: Three times a week.

Lucy: That sounds great.

Dialogue B

Rose: Lucy, you look so slim. How do you keep fit?

Lucy: I often take exercise at the gym.

Rose: What's your favorite sport?

Lucy: My favorite sport is playing badminton.

Rose: What other sports do you like?

Lucy: I also like playing table tennis! How about you?

Rose: So do I.

Lucy: Oh, really? Are you free tomorrow afternoon? Let's play table tennis.

Rose: Sure, I'm free. See you then.

Lucy: See you tomorrow.

Vocabulary

yoga	[ˈjəugə]	*n.*	瑜伽
slim	[slɪm]	*adj.*	苗条的，纤细的，细长的
gym	[dʒɪm]	*n.*	健身房；体育馆
favorite	[ˈfeɪvərɪt]	*adj.*	喜爱的，宠爱的，中意的
badminton	[ˈbædmɪntən]	*n.*	羽毛球
table tennis			乒乓球
by the sea			在海边
keep fit			保持健康
so do I			我也一样
See you then.			到时见。

Practice

1. Choose the best answer from the box to complete the dialogue.

A. Was it an exciting game?	B. Did you watch the football match last night?
C. Soon our team kicked another two goals.	D. What a pity!
E. What was the score?	

A: Hi!

B: Hi!

A: ____________

B: No, I missed it. By the time I got there, it had already finished.

A: ____________ It was a great football match.

B: ____________

A: Wow. It was a big score. We beat them 5∶3.

B: Really? That's amazing! ____________

A: Yeah. And I've never seen such an exciting match before! After 60 minutes, the American team was winning 3∶2.

B: Then what happened?

A: ____________

B: Great.

2. Finish the following dialogue according to the Chinese.

提示:Mary见到Anna,觉得她最近气色不错,Anna说她一直在健身房锻炼身体,喜欢游泳和打羽毛球,一周打三至四次,Mary说她也喜欢打羽毛球,并邀请Anna这个周末一起去健身房锻炼。

Mary: Hi, Anna, you look good recently.

Anna: Thank you.

Mary: How do you keep fit?

Anna: ____________.

Mary: What kind of sport do you like?

Anna: ____________.

Mary: How often do you take exercise every week?

Anna: ____________. And what's your favourite sport?

Mary: My favourite sport is playing badminton. ____________.

Anna: Good idea.

◈ Culture Corner

马拉松

马拉松(marathon)长跑是国际上非常普及的长跑比赛项目,全程距离为42.195千米(也有说法为42.193千米)。分全程马拉松(full marathon)、半程马拉松(half marathon)和四分马拉松(quarter marathon)三种。以全程马拉松比赛最为普及,一般提及马拉松,即指全程马拉松。

一、比赛规则

选手的身体情况需得到比赛医疗机构的认可，方能参加比赛。42.195 千米的距离对于人类来说，是一次对体能极限的挑战。在比赛中，运动员虽然也会从路边的小桌子或者是路边站立的人手中接过来一些水。但饮用水不是谁都可以随便递的。

在马拉松赛中，比赛的起点和终点都提供水和其他饮料，而在比赛路线上，每隔 2.5 千米有一个饮料站。水和饮料放在运动员经过时容易拿到的地方，运动员也可自备饮用水，并且可以在他们要求的地方设置饮料站。饮用水和湿海绵提供站设置在两个饮料站之间。在那里，长跑运动员和竞走运动员经过时可以取到饮用水，还可以从海绵中挤水冲洗头部，起到冷却作用。除此之外，运动员不能从比赛线路上其他地方获得饮料。

可以说，水是马拉松比赛中规定最为严格的部分。除此之外，运动员只要在裁判的监督下沿正确的路线比赛即可，如有特殊原因，还可在裁判员的监督下离开赛跑路线，但如果不在监督下离开就会失掉比赛资格。

二、运动魅力

马拉松的魅力之一，是比赛场地的开放。马拉松赛的场地多从城市道路选取，对参赛者来说，每跑一步、每过一段都是不同的风景。

马拉松的魅力之二，是对参赛者的包容。其他体育项目，只有同等选手才能同场竞技，业余爱好者几乎不可能与专业运动员比赛，而马拉松赛不同，无论专业运动员还是业余爱好者，都可以一起比赛。

马拉松的魅力显然不止两个，但不可否认，正是开放与包容这两个原因，让马拉松给人们带来了很多欢乐。

三、最好成绩

由于马拉松比赛一般在室外进行，不确定因素较多，所以在 2004 年 1 月 1 日前马拉松一直使用世界最好成绩，没有世界纪录。2004 年 1 月 1 日，国际田联宣布了一项新决定：包括马拉松在内的公路赛跑和竞走项目将告别只有世界最好成绩的时代，开始拥有世界纪录。

国际田联宣布这个决定后，英国长跑女将拉德克利夫被正式认定为女子 10 千米、20 千米和马拉松三个项目的世界纪录保持者，而波兰人科热日尼奥夫斯基则是男子 50 千米竞走的第一个世界纪录拥有者。

四、选手要求

（一） 身体条件

1. 身材不高、体重较小并非是不利条件
2. 胸围指数要大
3. 超群的呼吸循环系统
4. 肺活量与体重比要大
5. 强健的肠胃和肝脏

（二） 马拉松基础能力

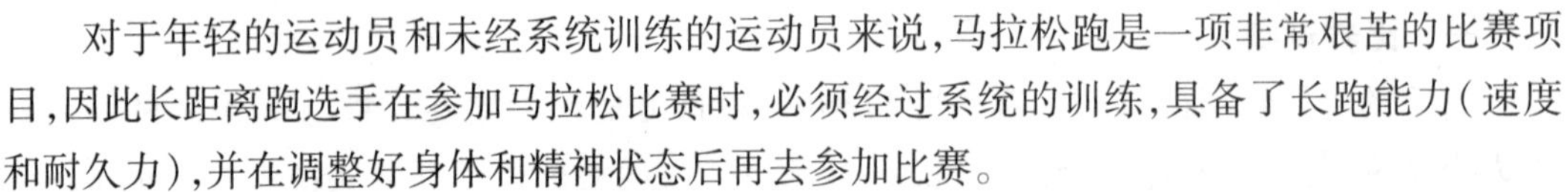

对于年轻的运动员和未经系统训练的运动员来说，马拉松跑是一项非常艰苦的比赛项目，因此长距离跑选手在参加马拉松比赛时，必须经过系统的训练，具备了长跑能力（速度和耐久力），并在调整好身体和精神状态后再去参加比赛。

（三） 马拉松精神力量

有人说："马拉松跑是孤独的竞赛，自己与自己斗争。"马拉松比赛不需要什么竞技用具，在比赛条件上是平等的，裁判是完全公平的，强者总是能够取胜。

精神力量不是天生就具备的东西，而是通过训练，作为后天的一种社会性而逐渐培养出来的，在马拉松比赛中精神力量占有很大的比重，是成为优秀选手的基本条件之一。

Section 3 Music

Warming-up

1. Play some classical English songs for students, and ask them the names of those songs.

2. Match the words or phrases with the correct pictures.

A. piano	B. conductor	C. Sydney Opera House	D. Grammy Award
E. guitar	F. headphone	G. flute	H. Central Conservatory of Music

a. ________

b. ________

c. ________

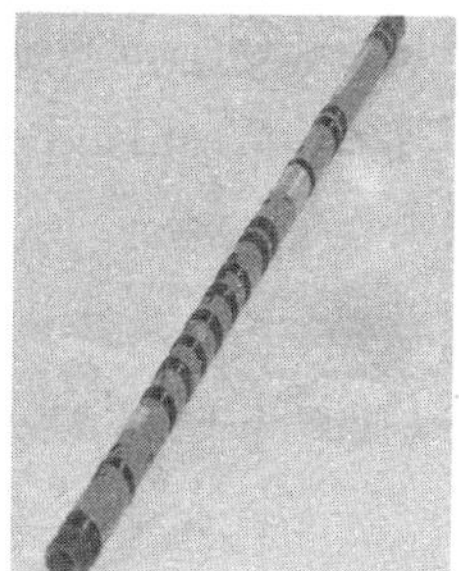

d. ________ e. ________ f. ________

g. ________ h. ________

Sentence Patterns

Partner A	Partner B
Do you like music?	I am tone-deaf.
Do you have a sweet voice?	I do well in singing.
What kind of music do you prefer?	Country music/R&B/Rock & Roll.
How about the rhythms of the music?	It sounds nice/fantastic.
Who is your favourite singer?	I can't keep with the fashion.
You can join us in singing.	It's so kind of you!

Communicating

Dialogue A

(*Jack and Peter are talking about their favourite singers.*)

Jack: Hi, Peter, how is everything going?

Peter: Not bad. You know I went to Jay's show last month.

Jack: Jay? You like him?

Peter: Yes, I like him very much.

Jack: Did you have a good time?

Peter: Of course. I am crazy about him. He has a gift for music.

Jack: What kind of songs did he sing in the concert?

Peter: R&B.

Jack: I think it was an unforgettable experience for you.

Peter: It certainly is.

Dialogue B

(*Mary meets her friend Amy on the playground.*)

Mary: Hey, what are you doing?

Amy: Oh, sorry, I'm listening to English songs on my phone.

Mary: What kind of music do you prefer?

Amy: I like country music, especially the rhythms of the music.

Mary: And who is your favourite singer?

Amy: Um, Paul Simon.

Mary: The same to me.

Vocabulary

show	[ʃʊu]	*n.*	表演;展览;显示;外观
gift	[gɪft]	*n.*	天赋;天资;赠品;礼物
unforgettable	[ˌʌnfəˈgetəbl]	*adj.*	难忘的
experience	[ɪkˈspɪəriəns]	*n.*	经历;经验;体验
prefer	[prɪˈfɜː]	*v.*	更喜欢;宁愿
rhythm	[ˈrɪðəm]	*n.*	节奏;韵律
have a good time			过得愉快;玩得痛快
be crazy about			对……疯狂;对……着迷
The same to me.			我也一样。

Practice

1. Finish the following dialogue according to the Chinese.

Susan: Good morning. Where did you go last night?

Peter: ________________(我和父母去听音乐会了).

Susan: Did you enjoy it?

Peter: Yes, very much.

Susan: ________________(你喜欢哪种类型的音乐)?

Peter: ________________(我最喜欢乡村音乐).

Susan: How about the rhythms of the music?

Peter: ________________(听起来很好).

Susan: ________________(你最喜欢的乡村歌手是谁)?

Peter: Taylor Swift.

2. Finish the following dialogue according to the Chinese.

提示:Lisa 见到 Nancy 不太高兴,问她怎么回事。Nancy 说她没能买到 Adele 在上海演唱会的门票感到非常失望。Nancy 告诉 Lisa,Adele 是她最喜欢的明星,Lisa 安慰她;她们交流后发现都喜欢 Jackson 的歌,希望有机会一起讨论一下。

Lisa: Hi, Nancy, ____________?

Nancy: Nothing!

Lisa: Come on, you can tell me.

Nancy: Well, I didn't get the ticket for Adele's show in Shanghai. When I went to buy the ticket ____________.

Lisa: Oh, ____________! Do you love her very much?

Nancy: Yes, ____________.

Lisa: Maybe next time.

Nancy: Thank you for your comforting. And ____________?

Lisa: My favourite singer is Michel Jackson.

Nancy: I also like him very much.

◈ Culture Corner

格莱美奖

格莱美奖(Grammy Awards),美国录音界与世界音乐界最重要的奖项之一,由录音学院(Recording Academy)负责颁发。学院由录音业的专业人士所组成,目的在于奖励过去一年中业界出色的成就。格莱美奖是美国四个主要音乐奖之一,相当于电影界的奥斯卡奖;另三个音乐奖分别为公告牌音乐奖、全美音乐奖和摇滚名人堂收录典礼。格莱美奖每年 2 月颁发,在公告牌和全美音乐奖后举行(这三个奖项称作"三大")。

一、奖项背景

"格莱美"(Grammy)是英文 gramophone(留声机)的变异谐音。以它命名的音乐奖迄今已有50多年历史，其奖杯形状如一架老式的留声机。

首届格莱美音乐奖于1958年颁发，以后录音学会每年举行一次颁奖仪式，奖项也由最初时的26项增加到28大类，共101项。美国当地时间2011年4月6日，美国录音艺术科学院宣布，2012年起将把格莱美奖奖项从原本的109个减为78个。

二、奖项地位

格莱美之所以能够为世界音乐人津津乐道，除了美国一直是全球流行音乐的中心，代表了流行音乐最高水平外，还有以下三个原因：

（一） 权威性（authority）

美国录音学会是一个由众多资深音乐人组成的机构，已在美国各地设置了12个地区分会和一个制作人与工程师分会，会员超过万人。歌唱家、演奏家、词作者、作曲家、指挥、摄影、解说词作者以及音乐录像片制作人等15类专业人员均可申请担任评委，但只有那些至少已有6件作品出版发行的人才有资格担任此职。没有真才实学和对音乐事业缺乏执着追求的人一般是进不了评委会的。

（二）公正性（justice）

格莱美奖的评选有一套十分严格的制度和程序。被推荐的作品必须选自当年。作品推荐上来后，首先要经过来自音乐界各领域的150多名专家筛选和资格确认，而后进行分类。除需由特别提名委员会投票的作品外，初选合格的作品要全部送交评委进行第一轮投票。但每个评委只能从其中挑选自己专精的9项进行投票，当然他们还要投票选出当年的年度唱片、年度专辑、年度歌曲和年度新人4个奖项。初评后的名单再交评委进行第二轮投票，每个评委的投票权除4个基本奖外，只能选择8个奖项进行投票。这些严格的措施有效地保证了评选的公正性。

（三） 广泛的影响性（influence）

第44届格莱美颁奖晚会就吸引了全球170个国家的约17亿观众收看。格莱美颁奖仪式走向世界，为格莱美音乐奖成为全世界音乐人广泛接受的一个奖项立下了汗马功劳。格莱美获奖作品显然不是少数人炒作或唱片公司自吹自擂的产物，而是经过专家和严格程序评选出来的。这些作品本身的高质量加上电视的宣传在使获奖者走红、唱片热卖的同时，也实实在在地起到了领导音乐潮流的作用。另一方面，评委们也是消费者，自然也会受到市场的影响，热卖唱片、走红歌手、流行电影歌曲当然也最容易走进他们的视野。

三、获奖纪录

派特·麦席尼和派特·麦席尼乐队共赢得过16次格莱美奖，包括连续6年6张不同专辑获奖。到2004年为止，麦席尼保持着跨类别最多奖项的纪录。

指挥乔治·萧提爵士是赢得格莱美奖最多之人，1997年逝世前他共获得32个奖项。

第52届格莱美奖颁奖典礼在2010年1月31日于美国洛杉矶的斯台普斯中心举行。其中，碧昂丝·诺利斯以十项提名和在一晚里夺下6项主要奖项最为人惊叹，也创下了格莱美奖女歌手单次获奖数量最多的新纪录。

2010年1月31日，泰勒·斯威夫特凭借专辑 *Fearless* 获得第52届格莱美奖的“年度专辑”奖,2016 年 2 月 16 日,美国流行女歌手泰勒·斯威夫特凭借专辑《1989》再次获得第 58 届格莱美奖的“年度专辑”奖,成为格莱美史上第一位两次获得年度专辑奖的女歌手。

Section 4 Movies

Warming-up

1. Match the types of films with the correct pictures.

A. romance	B. comedy	C. action	D. adventure
E. horror	F. war movie	G. science fiction	H. cartoon

a. ________

b. ________

c. ________

d. ________

e. ________

f. ________

g. ________

h. ________

2. Work in pairs as follows.

A: Do you like seeing films?

B: Yes.

Sentence Patterns

Talking about Movies
How about going to a movie tonight?
What kind of movies do you like?
How long will the film last?
What do you think of the film, Jane?
I'm a big fan of Western movies.
Who's the director of the movie?
The special effects in this movie are astonishing.
It's a great movie, but totally underappreciated.

Communicating

Dialogue A

(*Mike is now making a phone call to his friend Miller.*)

Mike: Hello! May I speak to Miller, please?

Miller: Hello, this is Miller speaking. Who is that, please?

Mike: This is Mike speaking. How have you been?

Miller: Just fine!

Mike: I called to ask if you are busy tomorrow evening.

Miller: Let me see. No, I don't think I've got anything planned. Why?

Mike: Well, I thought we might have dinner together and go to the cinema. There is a very good movie on in the local cinema.

Miller: What is the name of the movie?

Mike: *True Lie*.

Miller: Ah, it's really a wonderful film. I'd love to go.

Mike: I'll come and pick you up at six o'clock.

Miller: All right. See you then.

Dialogue B

(*Jack and Jane are talking about seeing a film.*)

Jack: I'm going to see a movie tonight. Would you like to join me?

Jane: Sounds great. What are you going to see?

Jack: *Vertical Limit.*

Jane: I want to see that movie for a long time. What time shall we go?

Jack: The movie starts at 7:30. Let's leave at 7:00.

Jane: All right.

Vocabulary

call	[kɔːl]	*vi.*	呼唤,喊叫;命令;打电话给
plan	[plæn]	*vt.*	计划,打算
movie	[ˈmuːvɪ]	*n.*	电影;电影院;电影业
local	[ˈləʊkəl]	*adj.*	地方的,当地的
sound	[saʊnd]	*vi.*	发声;听起来
make a phone			打电话
pick up			搭载;学会
Vertical Limit			《垂直极限》(电影名)

Practice

1. Finish the following dialogue according to the Chinese.

提示:Jackson 想请 Brown 先生去看电影,先问今天下午行不行,又问明天可否,定好见面的时间和地点后,两人分手。

Jackson: ____________ this afternoon? You see, there will be a nice film at the Victory Cinema.

Brown: That depends. What is it about?

Jackson: About the Civil War. *Gone with the Wind.*

Brown: Oh, I've seen it several times. By the way, I'll have to finish my homework by 5 o'clock.

Jackson: ____________ tomorrow afternoon? There will be another new film there.

Brown: A new film? That's great. What time will it be?

Jackson: At four o'clock. ____________ at a quarter to four.

Brown: All right. ____________? At the gate?

Jackson: Good. Let's make it. At the gate, at a quarter to four.

Brown: I'm afraid ____________. Bye!

Jackson: See you tomorrow afternoon.

2. Make up the rest of the dialogue according to the Chinese above.

Culture Corner

美国电影文化产业——好莱坞的大公司

在1900年的时候,好莱坞还只不过是离洛杉矶市中心十几千米的一个人口稀少的小镇。洛杉矶原来属于墨西哥,加利福尼亚被纳入美国版图后才成为美国的城市。1886年,房地产商哈维·维尔克特斯买下了这里的一块地,他的夫人将苏格兰运来的大批冬青树栽在这里,就有了好莱坞这个名字(在英语中,hollywood是冬青树的意思)。如今,好莱坞在美国文化中已经具有了重大的象征意义。诸如,日落大道、贝弗利山庄、圣费尔南多河谷、圣莫尼卡和马利布海滩等享有盛名的地方。可以说,好莱坞的发展史就是美国电影的发展史。

1907年,导演弗朗西斯·伯格斯带领他的摄制组来到洛杉矶,拍摄《基度山伯爵》。他们发现,这里明媚的自然风光、充足的光线和适宜的气候是拍摄电影的天然场所。从1909年开始,著名的制片人格里菲斯在好莱坞以天然背景拍摄了好几部影片。当时,美国电影的中心在东部,纽约是大本营。从此以后,许多电影公司纷纷来这里拍片,开始了美国电影业移师好莱坞的大转移。1912年起,许多电影公司在好莱坞落户。

一、 米高梅 (Metro-Goldwyn-Mayer, 简称 MGM)

1924年4月24日,世界电影史上的最大奇迹——米高梅(米特罗—高德温—梅耶的简称)电影公司宣告成立,并从此开始制造出一系列神话。

2001年,米高梅靠《汉尼拔》《律政俏佳人》的业绩得到4个多亿的票房收入,公司推出的其他影片则都不盈利。2002年,公司斥巨资投拍的战争大片《风语者》票房惨败,公司高层被迫辞职,米高梅再次进入被拍卖行列。

2005年4月8日,索尼公司以近50亿美元的价格将米高梅买下,从此,好莱坞八大公司中的最后一个独立制片公司消失了。如今,米高梅与哥伦比亚公司同属索尼旗下,开始了新的征程。

《猫和老鼠》

二、 派拉蒙公司(Paramount)

派拉蒙影业公司,以群星环绕雪山的标志为人所熟知。事实上,用高山来比喻派拉蒙在电影业的地位也是非常恰当的。在创立的最初30年,这家公司以众多的明星、高质量的影片和遍布全美的连锁影院，一直坐在好莱坞霸主的宝座上。

从1994年到2004年，派拉蒙进入了又一个兴盛期，出品了《勇敢的心》《阿甘正传》《泰坦尼克号》（与20世纪福克斯共同出资）《碟中谍》《变脸》《楚门的世界》和《拯救大兵瑞恩》这些名片。

2005年年底，派拉蒙收购了梦工厂。不过，这笔交易中并不包含梦工厂最能赚钱的部门——梦工厂动画，但对于这派拉蒙来说，仍旧意义重大，因为2004年前后，派拉蒙似乎迷失了方向，出品的电影很少有重磅炸弹级别的，而作为制片人的斯蒂文·斯皮尔伯格正好能为派拉蒙带来一批获利大的项目，其中最引人注目的当属《变形金刚》。

2008年10月派拉蒙与梦工厂正式分家，但仍会共同制作《变形金刚》系列。2012年，这家传奇式的电影公司迎来了100岁的生日。

《功夫熊猫》

三、20世纪福克斯公司(20th Century Fox)

20世纪福克斯电影制片公司，成立于1935年5月。在好莱坞的8家大公司中，20世纪福克斯是创立最晚的，而且经受的波折也最多，几次经历险些破产的厄运，创始人之一的威廉·福克斯虽然能够把姓氏写在公司名里，但实际上，在1935年这家公司正式挂牌时，威廉·福克斯已经是局外人。

20世纪福克斯的真正灵魂人物是达瑞尔·扎努克，这个热衷于制作巨片的电影大亨给20世纪福克斯打上了鲜明的印记，一说起福克斯，人们就会想起《最长的一天》《音乐之声》和《泰坦尼克号》这样大获成功的鸿篇巨制，当然，也有《埃及艳后》这样的票房臭蛋。而在摇摇欲坠的60年代之后，当澳大利亚的传媒业巨子鲁伯特·默多克伸手得到了接力棒，这家公司也进入了一个长达30年的稳定期，并支持年轻的乔治·卢卡斯拍出了《星球大战》系列电影。

《X战警》

四、华纳兄弟公司(Warner Brothers)

华纳兄弟娱乐公司(Warner Bros. Entertainment Inc.),或者简称华纳兄弟(Warner Bros.),是全球最大的电影和电视娱乐制作公司之一。目前,该公司是时代华纳旗下子公司,总部设于美国加利福尼亚的伯班克。

华纳兄弟包括几大子公司,包括华纳兄弟影业、华纳兄弟电视制作、华纳兄弟动画制作、华纳家庭录影、DC 漫画和 CW 电视网。

华纳兄弟成立于 1918 年,是美国成立时间第三悠久的电影公司,前两家为派拉蒙电影公司和环球影业,均成立于 1912 年。华纳兄弟娱乐公司的公司名称是为了纪念其四位创始人,即四位犹太人兄弟:哈利·华纳(1881—1958)、亚伯特·华纳(1883—1967)、山姆·华纳(1887—1927)以及杰克·华纳(1892—1978)。三位哥哥从 1903 年开始从事展映生意,并且买下了一台放映机,在宾夕法尼亚和俄亥俄的一些煤矿业城镇播放电影。1903 年,他们建立了他们的第一家电影院——位于宾夕法尼亚的纽卡索的 the Cascade(原来的电影院现在仍然保留了下来,作为纽卡索发展中的市中心的标志性建筑而被修复,希望吸引到更多游客)。到 1904 年,华纳兄弟成立了以匹兹堡为总部的 Duquesne Amusement & Supply Company(华纳兄弟影业公司的前身)发行电影。几年内,电影发行业务发展到了四个州。在第一次世界大战期间,他们开始尝试制作电影,并在 1918 年在好莱坞日落大道成立了华纳兄弟片厂。山姆和杰克·华纳负责制作电影,而哈利和亚伯特处理在纽约的财务和发行事宜。在 1923 年,他们正式合并为华纳兄弟影业公司。

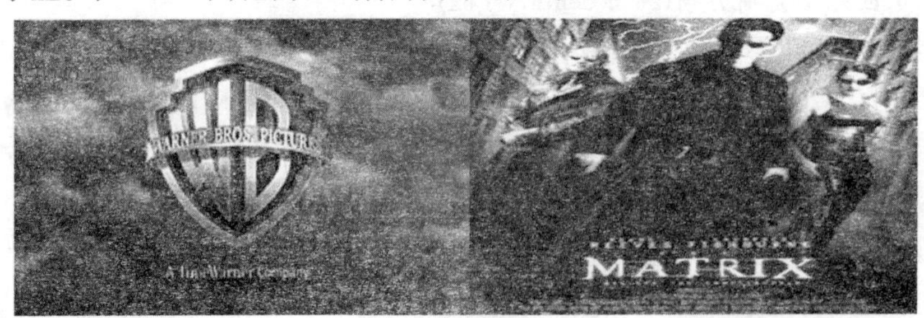

《黑客帝国》

五、迪士尼(The Walt Disney Company)

20 世纪三四十年代,依靠米老鼠起家的迪士尼并不是一家大公司,直到 1937 年,迪士尼的创始人华特·迪士尼才推出第一部长片《白雪公主与七个小矮人》。按观众人数来说,这部动画片是有史以来最卖座的影片之一。此后,迪士尼差不多每年拍摄一部动画长片,其中就有《皮诺曹》《幻想曲》《小飞象》和《小鹿斑比》。

从 21 世纪以来,迪士尼一直名列好莱坞顶级公司行列。2003 年,迪士尼出品了第一部 PG-13 级别的影片《加勒比海盗》,这标志着迪士尼将会更多地制作家庭电影以外的类型。2007 年,迪士尼成绩斐然,有《加勒比海盗 3:世界的尽头》《美食总动员》《国家宝藏 2》三部超级卖座片。

《疯狂动物城》

Section 5　Examinations

Warming-up

1. Look at the pictures below and work in pairs.

A. Are you afraid of taking a test?

B. Do you know how to get high scores in an exam?

2. Work in pairs as follows.

A: What did you get on the exam?

B: I only got …

Sentence Patterns

Failure	Success
He failed the exam because he didn't work hard.	Most students passed the examination.
My exam score is not good.	She sailed through her finals.
She took her failure in the examination to heart.	He got high marks in the final exam.
Many a student fails to pass on the exam.	He acquired an excellent grade in the final examination.
I lived in fear of failing my end-of-term exams.	Congratulations! You have passed the exam!

Communicating

Dialogue A

(*Bill, a student in a technical school, is talking with his classmate Tom about the Maths exam.*)

Bill: Hello.

Tom: Hi.

Bill: The Maths exam is over. How do you feel?

Tom: I'm a bit disappointed.

Bill: Why? What did you get on the exam?

Tom: I only got a C.

Bill: Oh! That's just above average.

Tom: Bill, I think your Maths is very good. Could you give me some advice on how to prepare for a test?

Bill: I just follow some simple study rules.

Tom: What rules? Could you explain them in detail?

Bill: Sure. First, listen to the teachers and take notes. Second, you have to work hard during the whole semester. Finally, I think the most important thing is to practise.

Tom: I see. So I should practise more and avoid the last-minute rush. Thank you for your advice. I guess I'd better study harder for the finals.

Bill: That's true. Good luck!

Tom: Thank you.

Dialogue B

(*Kate and Dick are talking about the examination.*)

Kate: How was the examination, Dick?

Dick: Not too bad. I think I passed the English and Maths. The questions were not very difficult. How about you?

Kate: The English and Maths papers weren't easy enough for me. I hope I haven't failed.

Dick: What I'm worrying about is Physics. Some of the questions were too difficult for me.

Vocabulary

disappointed	[ˌdɪsəˈpɔɪntɪd]	*adj.*	失望的，沮丧的
semester	[sɪˈmestə]	*n.*	学期
avoid	[əˈvɔɪd]	*vt.*	避免；避开，躲开
rush	[rʌʃ]	*n.*	匆忙，仓促
final	[ˈfaɪnl]	*n.*	期末考试
above average			平均以上
give sb. some advice			给某人一些建议
in detail			详细地
had better			最好
worry about			担心，担忧，烦恼

Practice

1. Finish the following dialogue according to the Chinese.

提示：原本擅长化学的 Cathy 考试时因漏做一页试题，正闷闷不乐时，这时遇见了 Mary。

Mary: Hi, Cathy, you don't look happy. ____________?

Cathy: I didn't do well in the Chemistry test.

Mary: Really? I could hardly believe it. Everyone knows you are ____________.

Cathy: But this time ____________.

Mary: What happened?

Cathy: I missed ____________.

Mary: What a pity! So ____________ next time!

Cathy: Yes, I will.

2. Make up the rest of the dialogue according to the Chinese above.

Culture Corner

(一)中国的考试制度

中国是世界上最早采用考试方法来甄别选拔人才的国家之一。从进士科举出现至科举废除,科举制在中国整整存在了1000多年。科举制对中国封建社会产生了重大的影响。它将衡量人才、选拔人才的权力集中到政府手中,有力地巩固了中央集权。

新中国的考试制度,经历了一个由考试到推荐再到考试的曲折发展的过程。"文革"中高考被废除,以贫下中农及单位的推荐代替考试,过分强调学生的政治素质而忽视业务素质,由此造成徇私舞弊和教育质量下降。1977年高考得以恢复。

现行考试制度也存在着一些弊端,比如,考试手段和考试内容的局限性。在当前教育改革的潮流中,考试制度面临着一次新的挑战,它未来的发展方向,必将通过改革来适应并推动教育的发展。

(二)美国高中教育及考试评价制度

美国是联邦制国家,各州在教育方面享有自治权,在中学教育体制及考试评价方面各有不同。

1. 美国中学的教育考试

最近几年,美国教育界出现了一个新的趋势:美国中学越来越重视考试,越来越多的州开始在中学实行更加规范、统一的考试制度。目前,美国中学的教育考试基本上分为三种类型:一是日常教学测验,二是学业水平测试,三是资格考试。

① 日常教学测验

这类考试是在日常的教学过程中进行的,十分频繁。一般在课堂教授的过程中或者是在一个学段、一个学期结束时进行。比如,西班牙语课堂时,一个小测验刚刚结束,剩余的课堂时间里学生在教师的许可下可以玩一种与西班牙语有关的游戏,学生的表现轻松自然,完全没有考试过后的不安。这一类考试成绩一般要记入学生平时成绩单,测验的目的主要是检测学生在某个阶段的学习情况,其功能主要是诊断教学过程中的得与失,发现教学中的问题,并促使教师、学生及时采取措施加以改善。

② 学业水平测试

学业水平测试的依据是各州制定的高中核心学习目标。20世纪90年代以来,美国各州开始制定高中核心学习目标,确定高中学生必须掌握的知识与技能,并作为高中学生学业评价的依据。美国多数州学业水平测试实行全州统一考试,另外还有不定期抽查式的全国统一考试。其主要功能是用于教育质量的检测和监控,以了解一个地区或全国学生的学业状况。《不让一个孩子落伍法》颁布后,为了提高学生的学业水平,采取全州统一学业水平测试的州越来越多。康州和加州每年都举行全州统一的学业水平测试。

全国高中教育水平测试,是一个全国性的抽查测试,用以分析、了解全国高中阶段的教育状况,美国每两年公布一次全国和各州的成绩报告单。2005年美国教育进展评鉴委员会对全国 50 个州的学生进行了抽样测试。测试结果表明，美国四年级和八年级学生都在数学方面取得了进步，但在阅读方面没有进步，甚至有所退步。据此国家教育政策中心需调整有关教育政策，促使地方采取有效措施提高学生学业水平。

③ 资格考试(各类升学的资格考试)

美国高中生升入大学需要 SAT(Scholastic Assessment Test，学术成绩测验)成绩，美国有很多家经过审定的权威考试机构，SAT 就是由这种非营利性考试服务机构主持的全国性考试，大学都承认其成绩，并将其作为必要条件之一。学生要进入大学，必须自己申请参加 SAT 考试，考试科目包括英语(阅读、写作)、数学两门课程，SAT 每年进行两次考试，学生在毕业之前可多次报名参加，考试成绩按最好的一次计算。美国的学生一般选择在 11 年级参加考试，学校也是自 11 年级开始有针对性地进行指导，成绩不理想的可在 12 年级重考。

2. 美国高校招生选拔考试

美国的高校选拔自主权在高校，政府不组织统一的选拔考试。在美国大学选拔新生一般依据五个方面：一是 SAT 成绩，二是高中阶段的学业成绩，三是教师的推荐信及学生本人的自荐信，四是学生的社交能力，五是 AP(Advanced Placement，大学学分先修课程)课程成绩。

① 美国的大学都在招生简章中公布录取新生的 SAT 标准。SAT 满分 1600 分，美国比较著名的大学 SAT 录取分数一般要在 1300 分以上，比如，哈佛大学要求学生 SAT 分数在 1480 分以上。根据学校的要求学生将自己最好的 SAT 成绩寄给大学，只要在大学规定的申请截止时间之前寄出，SAT 成绩都有效。

② 高中阶段的学业成绩主要是记入学生档案的过程评价性学业成绩，大学选拔时参照的主要是 11 年级成绩，也就是高中三年级时的成绩。

③ 每个学生都要向自己申请的大学寄去两位以上教师的推荐信和学生本人的自荐信。本人写的以选择这所大学的原因为主要内容的自荐信，在大学录取中非常重要，是录取人员首先要看的内容，每个学生还要附上两位以上教师的推荐信。只有在这些材料被认为符合标准之后，录取人员才再去查看学生的其他资料。

④ 学生的社交参与能力也是学校选拔新生的重要条件之一。学生要在自己的履历上写明参加过什么社团，担任过什么职务，做过多少义务工作。比如，到老人福利院去帮助老弱病残者，或者到医院、教会、基金会做义工，担任过学生会主席或者编辑过学生刊物等，这些都被看作学生能力的表现。美国大学非常重视学生的动手能力和实际交际能力。

⑤ 美国的高中普遍开设了大学承认学分的 AP 课程，在高中和大学课程之间建立了联系。准备进入大学的学生，多数在 12 年级选修 AP 课程和准备 AP 课程的测试，这是大学要求选修并考试的部分，一般一名学生最多选考 4 门，越是好的大学对这几门课程的要求越高，因此，学生都尽可能多修几门课程并考出好成绩，以便为进入理想的大学创造条件。

3. 对美国中学教育的思考

① 美国政府对教育极为重视，不仅重视对教育的投入，更重视教育质量的提高。在教学及评价过程中既强调统一的要求，又注重学生个性的培养及评价。

② 美国的教育发展速度极快，并且在发展过程中美国政府能够及时根据社会、经济发展的需要灵活、适时地调整教育政策以促进教育的发展。

③ 美国为了改变中学教育，特别是高中教育学业水平低下的现状，正在努力向中国等亚洲国家学习，加强考试在教育教学中的评价作用，且已初见成效，考试已促使学校和学生加强对文化课的学习。

④ 美国学生不是不考试或少考试，而是考试十分频繁，但从教师到学生不会唯考试是从，教学过程仍能按部就班地进行，能使考试很好地为他们的教与学服务。

⑤ 美国中学教育重视对学生动手能力等学术知识以外的能力的培养。不管是条件好的学校还是差的学校，农业机械室、工业机械模具室、动植物标本室、美术、音乐活动室等一类课室都被放在重要位置，占据了相当大的面积。

美国的教育也存在这样那样的问题，主要是因为发展不平衡，学生起点不同，特别是非英语母语的学生，要使他们也达到统一的标准，学校就必须对其进行辅导，否则他们很难通过考试。另外，由于州里确立的标准化测试与区里的毕业测试分离，考试次数过多、考试科目重复，学生感觉加重了负担，且由于州里统一举行的学业水平测试不计入学生档案，学生不予重视，迫使学校采取措施，比如，考试的当天为参加考试的学生提供免费早餐、个别辅导、有针对性的训练等。也有一些教师、家长和学生担心，在这种过于强调考试的风气之下，教师会不会不注重教书，而把重心放在训练学生如何应付考试上面。为执行《不让一个孩子落伍法》，各级教育管理部门还是以各自不同的方式在加强中学的考试评价。这似乎仍是美国教育改革不可逆转的趋向。

Module 5

Shopping for Girls

Shopping for Girls

Between the dead ring ash of extreme defense 极端防御的死灰环之间
The lonely groups of company boys 孤独的公司男孩
Snapping pictures of scrawny limbs and toothy grins 骨瘦如柴的四肢和露出牙齿的笑容
These are children riding naked on their tourist pals 赤身裸体地游荡者
While the hollows that pass for eyes swell from withdrawal 双眼因撤军而显得空洞
And he lies on a mattress in a rat infested room 躺在老鼠出没的房间的床垫上
Talking 'bout his family and the cold back home 谈论着家庭和回家
CHORUS
Between the dull cold eyes and the mind unstable 呆滞的冰冷的眼睛和心灵的不稳定之间
None over here reads the papers pal 没有人读报
'Tween the dull cold eyes and the mind unstable 呆滞的冰冷的眼睛和心灵的不稳定之间
He's a clean trick and he's shopping for girls 他是干净的，他在为女孩购物

Section 1 Shopping

Warming-up

1. Match the bills with the correct countries.

A. Germany	B. Italy	C. China	D. France	E. Spain
F. Russia	G. the US	H. Japan	I. the UK	

a. ________________

b. ________________

c. ________________

d. ________________

e. ________________

f. ________________

g. ________________

h. ________________

i. ________________

2. *Work in pairs as follows.*

A: Where/In which country is the bill often used?

B: It is often used in …

Sentence Patterns

Shop Assistant	Customer
May/Can I help you?	I'm looking for …
What can I do for you?	I'd like to have …
What size?	Oh, I'm just looking around.
What about the blue one?	Do you have a smaller one?
It's … *yuan*/dollars/pounds.	Can I try it on?
Here's your change.	How much is it/are they?
You can pay in cash/using a credit card.	How can I pay for it?

Communicating

Dialogue A

(It's going to be Anne's birthday. Her husband, Steve, wants to give Anne a big surprise. So he is looking around to choose a birthday present in a mall.)

Assistant: Can I help you, sir?

Steve: I'm looking for a suitable birthday present for my wife.

Assistant: I see. How about these earrings? Maybe they are perfect for your wife.

Steve: These yellow ones? But I don't think yellow is a good colour for her.

Assistant: Then what about the necklace? The blue one is of the latest style, and it's really beautiful.

Steve: Hmm, she likes the blue colour.

Dialogue B

Steve: This necklace looks fine. How much is it?

Assistant: It's $888.

Steve: Oh, I'll take it. And how can I pay for it, using a credit card or in cash?

Assistant: Either is OK, sir.

Steve: I know. Could you gift-wrap it for me?

Assistant: Certainly, sir. Your wife is a lucky lady!

Steve: Thank you. And I'm a lucky man!

Vocabulary

mall	[mɔːl]	*n.*	购物中心,商场
suitable	[ˈsjuːtəbl]	*adj.*	合适的,适当的
perfect	[ˈpɜːfekt]	*adj.*	完美的
latest	[ˈleɪtɪst]	*adj.*	最近的,最新的
cash	[kæʃ]	*n.*	现金,现款
gift-wrap	[ˈɡɪftræp]	*vt.*	用美丽的纸张及缎带包装
give sb. a surprise			给某人一个惊喜
look around			到处逛逛
look for			寻找
be perfect for			十分合适的
a credit card			一张信用卡
pay in cash			现金支付

Practice

1. Finish the following dialogue according to the Chinese.

提示:Bob 想买一件 L 码的毛衣。售货员建议他买件红色的,可他说不喜欢红色的。售货员就推荐买件蓝色的,试穿后他觉得不错。得知蓝色的价格是 45 元,比红色的还便宜 5 元,他就刷卡买下了。

Salesgirl: Good morning, sir. ____________?

Bob: Good morning. ____________.

Salesgirl: ____________?

Bob: Size L.

Salesgirl: Here are many types of sweaters. ____________?

Bob: But I don't like red.

Salesgirl: Would you like the blue one?

Bob: It looks nice ... but ____________?

Salesgirl: Certainly. Here is the changing-room.

2. Make up the rest of the dialogue according to the Chinese above.

Culture Corner

(一) 文明购物

日常生活中离不开购物,因此了解一些购物礼仪,做到文明购物是很有必要的。

- 到柜台前购物时,首先要有礼貌地与营业员打招呼,然后详细说明购物要求。如果营业员正在为别的顾客服务,不要高声喊叫,更不能敲击柜台,而应该耐心等待。最后,对营业员的热情、周到的服务要表示感谢。
- 在自选商场购物时,要自觉遵守商场的各项购物规定,例如,不大声喧哗、不推搡哄抢、注意环境卫生等。挑选商品时要注意轻拿轻放,不要故意损坏或弄脏物品。如不小心损坏了商品,要主动赔偿。
- 购物缴款时,有两人以上等待结账就应该自觉排队,并注意与他人保持一定距离,以免给他人造成不便。

(二) 美国的购物方式

在美国,购物有多种方式,比较有代表性的有以下几种:

- 99 店(99 only stores):这种商店介于便利店(convenience store)和超级市场(supermarket)之间,主要销售日常生活用品和食品。其销售策略是每件东西售价均为 99 美分。
- 专业店(specially store):在这些商店里,一方面是同一类产品可以选择的范围比较广,另一方面是具有丰富专业知识的销售人员可以为你提供更优质的服务。

- 大型购物中心(shopping center/shopping mall):这些购物中心多位于城郊地,规模大,一般都拥有足够的停车位,几十家、上百家各种各样的百货店、卖场以及专业连锁零售店,集购物、休闲、娱乐、餐饮活动于一体。
- 厂家直销店(factory store):在美国,最有名的厂家直销店为 Outlets,在这里,聚集了 Hugo Boss,Polo,Levis,Gucci,Burberry 等品牌专卖店。许多商品以低于商场零售价 30% ~50% 的价格出售。
- 旧货市场(flea market,yard sale,garage sale):比较大的旧货市场称为 flea market(跳蚤市场),一般都有固定的场所,每个月开业一天。

(三)怎么将外汇兑换人民币最划算?

A 先生、B 先生、C 先生在同一天将各自银行账户中的 1000 欧元兑换成人民币,然而三人得到的人民币金额却相差不少,A 先生得到了 10631.80 元人民币,B 先生得到了 10723.10元人民币,C 先生却到了 10794.57 元。最多和最少之间相差了 162 元多!

是银行工作人员出错了么?

并不是。那是因为将手中的外汇兑换成人民币是有学问的,不同换法得到的结果会完全不同。

一、 汇钞有别

在我国,居民外币储蓄存款有两种账户:现钞户和现汇户。如果存入的是外币现钞,则为现钞存款;如果外币资金是从境外或港澳台地区汇入,或携入的外币票据(如旅行支票、私人支票)转存款账户,则为现汇存款。外币现汇在银行的人民币牌价是高于外币现钞的。上述案例中,A、B、C 三人本都是现汇户。然而韩先生在兑换前却先将 1000 欧元支取出来再兑换成人民币,使“现汇”变成了“现钞”,因此在兑换人民币时适用银行当天的“欧元钞买价”1063.18 元/100 欧元;而 B 先生直接将现汇户中的欧元兑换成人民币,使用的是银行当天的“欧元汇买价”1072.31 元/100 欧元,于是两人所得就差了 90 多元人民币。

二、 利用汇率波动可获取更多兑换所得

我国是汇率管制的国家,每天由人民银行公布当天的人民币牌价。在一天中,各种外币对人民币的牌价是相对固定的,但在国际外汇市场上,各币种之间的汇率波动却是随时发生的。目前内地居民进入国际汇市的渠道就是银行提供的即时外汇交易服务,如中行的“外汇宝”。市民完全可以使用“外汇宝”转换手中货币的币种,从而提高其对人民币的“相对价值”。精明的李先生就是先做了一个“外汇宝”交易,用当时的汇率卖掉 1000 欧元现汇,买入 1306.2 美元现汇,再用当天银行的美元“汇买价”826.41 元/100 美元换到了 10794.57 元人民币。

因此,日常生活中我们应该注意:

- 如非必需,现汇存款不要轻易支取,否则会让手中的外汇“贬值”。每年春节前夕,总有大量“赡家款”从境外汇入境内,通常有电汇和票汇两种方式,直接转入存款都是现汇。
- 有外汇存款的市民不妨开通“外汇宝”功能,在汇率波动时通过转换货币而让存款

"升值"。中行"外汇宝"通过柜面、电话、网上银行、自助设备都可进行交易,相当方便。

Section 2 Ordering Dishes

Warming-up

1. Match the common food with the correct pictures.

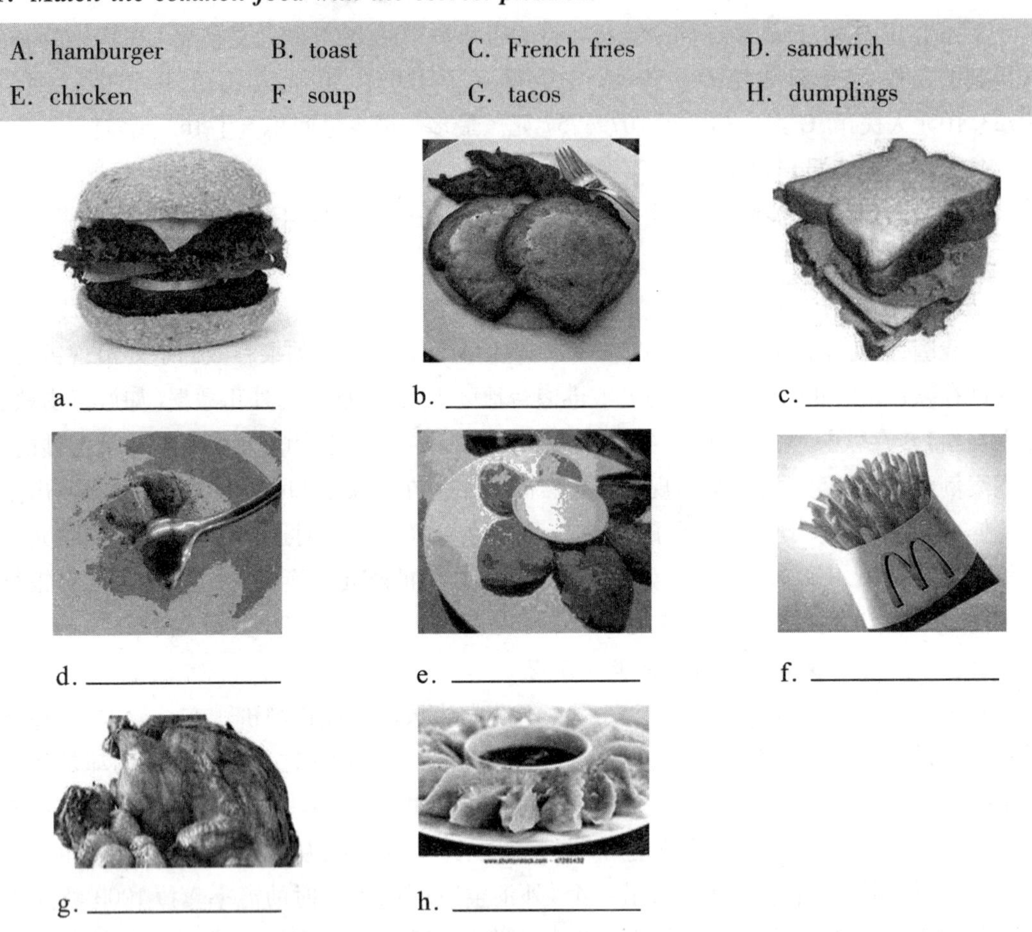

A. hamburger	B. toast	C. French fries	D. sandwich
E. chicken	F. soup	G. tacos	H. dumplings

a. ________ b. ________ c. ________

d. ________ e. ________ f. ________

g. ________ h. ________

2. Work in pairs as follows.

A: What do you usually have for breakfast/lunch/dinner?

B: I usually have … for breakfast/lunch/dinner.

◈ Sentence Patterns

Customer	Waiter
I want to go to a restaurant with reasonable price?	It's on me today.
May I order, please?	We have a daily chef's special of fried chicken.
What do you have for today?	Let's go to the Han Yuan Hotel. The price there is reasonable.
Do you have a reservation?	Yes. The reservation is under Miss Lin.
Could I have the check?	Yes. What would you like to start with?

◈ Communicating

Dialogue A

(*Order dishes.*)

A: Are you ready to order now?

B: I'd like to see the menu. What do you have for today?

A: We have a daily chef's special of fried chicken.

B: I'd like to have something spicy today.

A: Would you like spicy steak? It's very delicious.

B: Really? I'd like to try.

A: Anything else?

B: Yes, I'll try some lobster, and give me some green salad together.

A: OK.

Dialogue B

(*Order a seat.*)

A: Good evening. Do you have a reservation?

B: Yes. The reservation is under Miss Li.

A: Miss Li. This way, please.

B: Thank you.

A: You're welcome. I'll be with you right away to take your order.

B: What do you recommend?

A: Special of the beer steak.

B: OK. I'd like it.

A: Very good. I'll bring you your appetizer immediately.

Vocabulary

chef	[ʃef]	*n.*	厨师，大师傅
lobster	[ˈlɒbstə]	*n.*	龙虾；龙虾肉
steak	[steɪk]	*n.*	牛排；肉排；鱼排
reservation	[ˌrezəˈveɪʃn]	*n.*	保留；预订，预约；保留地，专用地
appetizer	[ˈæpɪtaɪzə(r)]	*n.*	开胃品
immediately	[ɪˈmiːdiətli]	*adv.*	立即，马上；直接地

Practice

1. Finish the following dialogue according to the Chinese.

提示：顾客去饭店吃饭，服务员请顾客看今天的菜单，顾客说要牛排。服务员问顾客牛排要几成熟，顾客回答八成熟。服务员问是否要配菜沙拉，顾客说不需要了。服务员说将很快将开胃菜送过来。

A：Have you had time to ____________ the menu（菜单）?

B：Er, yes. I ____________ the beef steak（牛排）.

A：____________ would you like your meat cooked（几成熟）?

B：____________ ,please.

A：Would you like a side salad（配菜沙拉）?

B：No, ____________.

A：____________. I will bring your appetizer immediately.

2. Finish the following dialogue according to the Chinese.

在一家餐厅，服务员先向客人打招呼，问是否预订了餐桌，把客人领到座位上后，询问客人是否看菜单预备点菜。顾客问有什么特色菜，服务员说有一个厨师的特色菜“油炸鸡”。

A：Good evening. Have you booked a table?

B：Yes, a table near the window.

A：____________, ____________ please.

B：Thank you. ____________ ?

A：Here's the menu.

B：____________?

A：We have a daily chef's special of fried chicken.

Culture Corner

（一）美国餐馆

美国餐馆大致可以分为以下几种：

如果你想吃汉堡、热狗或者是炸土豆条，你可以去 refreshment stand（点心铺）或者 snack bar（小吃店）。这类摊点不仅有吃的，还卖饮料，而且到处都可以找到。想去环境好一点的，建议可以去 fast-food chains（快餐连锁店）。

如果想吃比萨，可以去 pizza stand（馅饼摊），如果你坐在餐桌前吃，吃完了，别忘了付点小费。

如果要吃三明治，luncheonette（便餐店）是不错的选择，在这种小店里吃饭非常实惠。如要吃蔬菜，大街上的 salad bar（沙拉酒吧）里有供应。

如果要享受西餐的全套饭菜，可以去两个地方：一是 diner（小餐馆），另一类是 coffee shop（咖啡店）。

（二）西方餐桌礼仪常识

西餐不像中餐，每个人都是单独一盘食物，从最开始的沙拉到最后的甜点，并不是自由取食，而是由服务员一轮一轮地给各位上菜，英文中称食物为 course，主食为 main course。开始吃时，一定要等到大家面前都有食物摆放好，如果别人邀请到家吃，等主人先吃。为了表示礼貌，最好所有人都能够同步用餐，大家一起吃沙拉，吃完服务员收走，再一起吃主食。

进餐时，餐盘在中间，那么刀子和勺子放置在盘子的右边，叉子放在左边。一般右手写字的人，吃西餐时，很自然地用右手拿刀或勺，左手拿叉，杯子也用右手来端。

在桌子上摆放刀叉，一般最多不能超过三副。三道菜以上的套餐，必须在摆放的刀叉用完后随上菜再放置新的刀叉。

刀叉是从外侧向里侧按顺序使用（也就是说事先按使用顺序由外向内依次摆放）。

进餐时，一般都是左右手互相配合，即一刀一叉成双成对使用。也有例外，喝汤时，则只把勺子放在右边——用右手持勺。食用生牡蛎一般也是用右手拿牡蛎叉食用。

刀叉有不同规格，按照用途不同而决定其尺寸的大小也有区别。吃肉时，不管是否要用刀切，都要使用大号的刀。吃沙拉、甜食或一些开胃小菜时，要用中号刀。叉或勺一般随刀的大小而变。喝汤时，要用大号勺，而喝咖啡和吃冰激凌时，则用小号为宜。

Section 3 Food

Warming-up

1. Match the food with the correct pictures.

A. meat	B. hamburger	C. banana	D. egg
E. rice	F. noodle	G. lobster	H. grape

a. ________

b. ________

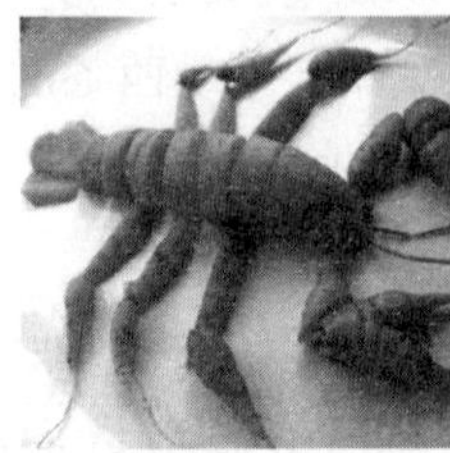

c. ________

d. ________

e. ________

f. ________

g. ________

h. ________

2. Work in pairs as follows.

A: What's your favourite food?

B: It's …

Sentence Patterns

Asking about the Food	Possible Responses
What's your favourite food?	I like ... best.
Would you please give me some advice on ...?	My favourite food is ...
What do you eat for lunch?	I often have rice with some vegetables.
What about some bananas?	All right.
What do you think of Chinese food?	It's delicious.

Communicating

Dialogue A

(*Tom is talking with Mary about food.*)

Tom: What are we going to eat for dinner?

Mary: I'm going to cook some chicken.

Tom: I'm afraid the chicken is rotten.

Mary: But I just bought it the day before yesterday.

Tom: Well, I forgot to put it in the fridge. Why can't we go out for dinner?

Mary: OK. Let's go.

Dialogue B

(*Billy is at a restaurant now.*)

Waiter: Are you ready to order now?

Billy: Yes, I'll have some salad, beef and some potatoes.

Waiter: How do you want the beef, rare, medium or well-done?

Billy: Well-done, please.

Waiter: Anything to drink?

Billy: I'd like a cup of tea.

Waiter: OK.

Vocabulary

beef	[biːf]	*n.*	牛肉
medium	[miːdiəm]	*adj.*	适中的
I'm afraid …			恐怕……
be ready to do sth.			准备做某事
go out for dinner			出去吃晚饭
anything to drink			喝点什么

Practice

1. Finish the following dialogue according to the Chinese.

提示:Jack 遇到 Sue 发现他的脸色不太好,询问得知是由于变胖了,于是建议他减肥。Sue 请他说得详细点,Jack 告诉 Sue 要小心饮食,最好不要吃太多的糖和油炸食品,还建议他多锻炼,但是 Sue 说他没有时间,整天都在忙于工作,因此 Jack 建议他步行去上班,因为他家靠近办公室。Sue 认为这个建议很好并表示了感谢。

Jack: You don't look well. ____________?

Sue: It's my weight. I am ____________.

Jack: I suggest you should lose weight.

Sue: ____________?

Jack: You should be careful with your food.

Sue: ____________?

Jack: Yes. You'd better stop eating ____________. I also think you should ____________.

Sue: I see. But I haven't got the time.

2. Make up the rest of the dialogue according to the Chinese above.

Culture Corner

食物与健康的关系

要获得人体所必需的各种营养素,必须注意食品的合理搭配,切忌吃荤不吃素或吃素不吃荤。同时,合理的搭配亦能提高蛋白质的生理价值,因为各种蛋白质是由多种氨基酸组成的,甲蛋白质所缺乏的某种氨基酸恰为乙蛋白质所含有,乙蛋白质所缺乏的恰为甲蛋白质所含有。孩子中的偏食、精食问题相当突出。一方面,偏吃甜食、零食,对“粗茶淡饭”不屑一顾,而对自己喜爱的食物则乐此不疲。另一方面,食物过于精细,精米、精面、精制糕点……

使胃肠永远处于“幼稚”状态。这么一来，膳食结构失去平衡，很容易造成维生素、纤维素、矿物质、微量元素缺乏而致病，同时抵抗力下降也容易使身体受细菌、病毒入侵而生病。

改变不良饮食习惯对健康大有好处，但做起来并不容易，因为所谓习惯成自然，积习久之，积重难返。要下点决心才行。在培养良好饮食习惯的同时，对原来不良的习惯应有所认识，然后改变。不要吃太热的食物，稍微等一会儿，待其凉些入口并不费事。专家认为，不要长久或大量食用腌制食品或含有大量添加剂的食品，使有害化学物质不易达到对人体构成损害的程度，也可让身体来得及清除有害物质。家长对孩子饮食的考虑要全面些，在餐桌上不应由孩子说了算。另外进食时，要有足够的时间和心情对食物去咀嚼、品味，这样有助于消化。

怎样才算饮食不当呢？这是指对饮食数量的多少、质量的优劣和卫生条件的好坏的掌握和处理不当，而给身体健康带来了各种不良影响。饮食不当包括三方面：一是经常饮食不足或者太差，二是经常饮食过量或者太好，三是饮食不卫生或者吃了变质的食物。经常饮食不足或者太差，对身体有什么危害呢？我们知道，人体每天都要摄取一定量的蛋白质、脂肪、碳水化合物、维生素、矿物质、水和粗纤维来维持人体生命活动的需要。如果这些营养素供给的数量不足或者质量太差，都可能使人生病，至于生什么病就要看缺乏什么营养素了，通常称这类疾病为营养缺乏病。

以蛋白质缺乏病为例。引起蛋白质缺乏病的原因较多，可能由于饮食中长期缺少蛋白质，而引起营养性的水肿。可能由于偏食或者所食用的蛋白质的质量不好，缺乏某些必需的氨基酸，而引起脱发。也可能由于儿童、孕妇和乳母所需要的蛋白质量特多，而在饮食上没有注意补充或增加，导致蛋白质的摄入不足。还可能由于各种肠道疾病或其他疾病，导致影响食欲，对蛋白质的消化、吸收不良。

缺乏蛋白质的病，主要是由于血浆蛋白质的浓度降低，而引起由下肢开始渐及上身发生水肿。甚至还可能出现心悸、全身乏力、形体消瘦、体重减轻和发育不良等症状。这样由于机体抵抗力降低，往往容易感染疾病。治疗蛋白质缺乏病的办法，是在饮食中适当地增加蛋白质。蛋白质有动物蛋白质和植物蛋白质之分，一般动物蛋白质如鱼类、肉类、蛋类和乳制品等，所含各种必需氨基酸，它的营养价值较高。植物蛋白质以黄豆为佳，而小麦、玉米和薯类所含的必需氨基酸不够完全或者某几种含量较少，不能作为补充蛋白质缺乏病的首先食物。但是只要把这些植物蛋白质混合食用，也可以互相补偿，增加营养价值，不一定非要采用动物蛋白质不可。

一般来说，成人每日进食蛋白质为 80 克左右（约为 60 克瘦猪肉或两个鸡蛋中所含的蛋白质量），就能满足人体的需要了，但体力劳动者、某些消耗性疾病的患者以及处于生长发育旺盛时期的青少年，蛋白质的需要量就要适当的增加了。另外，对某些蛋白质缺乏严重的病人，可在医生指导下注射适量的水解蛋白质溶液，加以矫正。

Module 6

Heal the World

Heal the World

There's a place in your heart 在你心里有个地方
And I know that it is love 我知道那就是爱
And this place could be much 这个地方可比明天
Brighter than tomorrow 更加绚烂
And if you really try 如果你真去尝试
You'll find there's no need to cry 你将发现无须哭泣
In this place you'll feel 在这里你不会感到
There's no hurt or sorrow 悲痛与伤害
There are ways to get there 通往那里的路很多
If you care enough for the living 只要你对生命足够关怀
Make a little space 留一个小小的空间
Make a better place ... 创造一个更好的地方……
Heal the world 治愈这个世界
Make it a better place 创造一个更好的地方
For you and for me 为你我
And the entire human race 为全体人类
There are people dying 有人濒临死亡
If you care enough for the living 如果你对生命足够关怀
Make it a better place 创造一个更好的地方
For you and for me 为你我
If you want to know why 如果你想知道缘由
There's love that cannot lie 那就是爱从不撒谎
Love is strong 爱强大有力
It only cares of joyful giving 只关心欢乐的付出

If we try we shall see 试着去爱，我们将看到

In this bliss we cannot feel 在爱的庇佑里感觉不到

Fear or dread 害怕或恐惧

We stop existing and start living 我们不再仅仅只是生存，而将开始生活

Then it feels that always 让爱常存

Love's enough for us growing 伴随成长

So make a better world 一个更好的世界

Make a better place ... 一个更好的地方……

Heal the world 治愈这个世界

Make it a better place 创造一个更好的地方

For you and for me 为你我

And the entire human race 为全体人类

There are people dying 有人濒临死亡

If you care enough for the living 如果你对生命足够关怀

Make it a better place 创造一个更好的地方

For you and for me 为你我

And the dream we were conceived in 我们的梦想

Will reveal a joyful face 将显现快乐的面容

And the world we once believed in 曾信仰过的世界

Will shine again in grace 重新优雅放光

Then why do we keep strangling life 那为何我们还要扼杀生命

Wound this earth, crucify its soul 伤害这个地球，在十字架上钉死它的灵魂

Though it's plain to see 尽管如此显然

This world is heavenly 这个天堂般的人间

Be god's glow 仍是上帝的荣光

We could fly so high 我们可以高高飞翔

Let our spirits never die 让灵魂长生不老

In my heart I feel you are all my brothers 在我心中你们皆是我的兄弟

Create a world with no fear 创造一个无畏的世界

Together we cry happy tears 我们一起含着幸福的泪水

See the nations turn their swords into plowshares 喜看国家与国家化干戈为玉帛

We could really get there 我们真的能达到梦想

If you cared enough for the living 只要你足够关怀生命

Make a little space 留个小小的空间

To make a better place ... 创造一个更美好的地方……

Heal the world 治愈这个世界

Make it a better place 创造一个更好的地方
For you and for me 为你我
And the entire human race 为全体人类
There are people dying 有人濒临死亡
If you care enough for the living 如果你对生命足够关怀
Make it a better place 创造一个更好的地方
For you and for me 为你我
Heal the world 治愈这个世界
Make it a better place 创造一个更好的地方
For you and for me 为你我
And the entire human race 为全体人类
There are people dying 有人濒临死亡
If you care enough for the living 如果你对生命足够关怀
Make it a better place 创造一个更好的地方
For you and for me 为你我
Heal the world we're living 治愈我们所生活的世界
Save it for our children 为我们的下一代保存它的美丽

Section 1 Weather

Warming-up

1. Match the common weather conditions with the correct pictures.

A. cloudy	B. windy	C. sunny	D. lightning
E. rainy	F. foggy	G. snowy	H. hot

a.  ________ b.  ________ c. ________

d. ______________ e. ______________ f. ______________

g. ______________ h. ______________

2. ***Work in pairs as follows.***

A: What's the weather like today?

B: It's ...

Sentence Patterns

Asking about the Weather	Possible Responses
What's the weather like today?	It's cloudy/windy/sunny/hot/dry.
What's it like outside?	It's bad outside.
How hot is it?	It's about 35 degrees above zero.
A lovely day, isn't it?	A lovely day indeed.
What's the weather forecast tomorrow?	It's going to be rainy tomorrow.

Communicating

Dialogue A

(*Jack is talking about weather with Mary.*)

Jack: Beautiful day, isn't it?

Mary: Yes. It's not like what the radio said at al.

Jack: I wish it would stay this way for the weekend.

Mary: As long as it doesn't snow!

Jack: I agree with you.

Dialogue B

(*You are talking about weather with Joan.*)

You: What's the weather like today?

Joan: It's sunny, but it's a little windy.

You: What's the temperature then?

Joan: About 19 centigrade.

You: Oh, it's good for the basketball match.

Joan: Sure.

Vocabulary

weather	[weðə]	*n.*	天气
weekend	[ˈwiːkend]	*n.*	周末
temperature	[ˈtemprətʃə]	*n.*	温度,体温
centigrade	[ˈsentgreɪd]	*n.*	摄氏
not ... at all			一点也不
stay this way			像这样
as long as			只要
a little windy			有点儿风
be good for			有利于

Practice

1. Finish the following dialogue according to the Chinese.

提示:Lily 和 Jane 早晨在街上遇见,她们相互问候。Lily 说今天天气不错,Jane 表示赞同,但是提出有点儿热。Lily 说昨天下了雨,所以昨天天气很凉爽。Jane 说她的家乡华南的夏季与这里类似。Lily 更喜欢英国的天气,不会这么热,但是总是下雨,这可能有点烦人。Jane 认为她说得很有道理。

Lily: ____________, Jane.

Jane: Good morning, Lily.

Lily: It's a nice day, right?

Jane: Pretty good, but it's ____________?

Lily: Yes. It rained yesterday, and it was quite cool.

Jane: Summer in my hometown in South-China ____________.

2. Make up the rest of the dialogue according to the Chinese above.

Culture Corner

英国人为何总是谈论天气

我们都知道,英国人总是在谈论天气,谈话的开始往往总是对天气一番评论。是不是大家没话找话?又或是什么我们没有注意到的原因?一个国家民众的习惯总是会有它一定的原因的,让我们来好好研究下吧!

一、天气使然,让人难以忽略啊!

英国多变的天气催生出了许多对于天气的描写,一串一串对于天气的词汇句子让人不难想象为啥英国人总是喜欢谈论天气。

二、咱也没啥侃的,要不,侃侃天气?

有这么一个关于英国人谈论天气的小故事,萧伯纳有一次在散步时遇到个老先生,老先生跟他打招呼说:Good afternoon, Mr. Shaw! It's such a lovely day, isn't it?(下午好萧伯纳先生,今儿个天气真是不错啊!)萧伯纳回答道:Oh, yes. But twenty people have told me about it in the past two hours. Thank you.(是啊,但是两个小时里已经有20个人跟我这么说了啊。谢谢你。)

三、西方文化与习惯

在英语中,weather与climate有着不同的意义。weather指天气,climate指气候。欧美人见面时常常喜欢谈论天气,英国人尤其如此。天气是个谈不尽、讲不烦的话题,人人擅长此道。英国大文豪狄更斯笔下的英国绅士的形象:高礼帽、燕尾服和雨伞。这足见英国人对天气的重视。这或许是因为英国的天气历来变化无常,天气好坏给人们生活带来直接影响。况且天气是一个不涉及个人私事的中性话题。欧美人士不大愿意和外人谈私事,因此天气便在茶余饭后给人们提供了有趣的话题。在公共场合与陌生人开始交谈时,谈天气可以是一种既有用又不会得罪人的活跃气氛、开始对话、结交朋友的方式。

四、谈天技巧

与人以天气为话题交谈,也要讲究点策略。一般是先打招呼,比如,以Hello或Hi开始,再进行交谈就较容易。如果一上来就用"Lovely day, isn't it?"就显得生硬了一点。由天气过渡其他话题也要自然。

评论天气不要反驳。只要有人说"Lovely day, isn't it?"(天气不错,是吗?)你就要毫不犹豫地回答:Oh, yes. It's great.(是啊!真是太好了。)

五、东西方文化与习惯差异

在外国,如果在公园里一位绅士想认识坐在邻座的漂亮女孩,他会轻轻走过去,微笑着说:"Hello, lovely day, isn't it?"对方通常会礼貌地回答:"Yes, I hope the good weather will stay."这时,进一步的交流可以说是水到渠成、顺理成章了。但在中国,如果一位男士突然用同样的方式对邻座的女孩大声地说一句:"好天气哟!"那么一定会被认为神经病。由此可见,东西方文化存在巨大差异。

Section 2 Environment

Warming-up

1. Match the words or phrases with the correct pictures.

A. noise pollution	B. forest destruction	C. water pollution
D. air pollution	E. food pollution	F. litter

a. ________________

b. ________________

c. ________________

d. ________________

e. ________________

f. ________________

2. Work in pairs as follows.

A: What's the biggest environment problem in your city?

B: Air pollution.

Sentence Patterns

Our world is now becoming worse and worse. What's the biggest environment problem in your country? Pollution has caused many diseases. Are you doing anything to help the environment? We are taking some steps to protect our environment. I want to help out the environment. I turn off the lights when I leave the room, so we can conserve more energy. My friend and I are going to pick up litter today. I'm going to ride my bike around more often, so I save money on gas and pollute less often. That's cool. Maybe I'll do the same.

Communicating

Dialogue A

(*Judy meets Kenny in the garden in the afternoon.*)

Judy: Good afternoon!

Kenny: Good afternoon!

Judy: What are you doing, my friend?

Kenny: We are picking up litter in the grass.

Judy: Pollution has caused many problems.

Kenny: Everyone should protect the environment.

Judy: I also want to help out the environment.

Kenny: That's great!

Dialogue B

(*Jack and Kate are talking about environmental problems in their city.*)

Jack: Environmental problems in our city are becoming worse and worse.

Kate: In your opinion, what's the biggest environmental problem in our city?

Jack: I think it is the air pollution.

Kate: It's time for us to do something to protect our environment.

Jack: What should we do?

Kate: For example, we can use public transport instead of driving our cars.

Jack: That's good!

Vocabulary

litter	[ˈlɪtə(r)]	*n.*	杂物;垃圾
pollution	[pəˈluːʃn]	*n.*	污染
cause	[kɔːz]	*vt.*	导致;引起
protect	[prəˈtekt]	*vt.*	保护;保卫
environmental	[ɪnˌvaɪrənˈmentl]	*adj.*	环境的
transport	[ˈtrænspɔːt]	*n.*	运输
pick up			拾起,捡起;学会
that's great			太棒了
in one's opinion			按照某人的观点
for example			例如

Practice

1. Finish the following dialogue according to the Chinese.

提示:Peter 给 Lily 看了几张关于环境污染的图片,他认为空气污染最为严重,Lily 说,城市的环境越来越糟糕,污染导致了很多人生病,Peter 提出帮助改善环境的想法,Lily 表示赞同,并准备以后骑自行车上班,Peter 打算以后出行用公共交通设施。

Peter: Lily, look at these pictures: Dark dense smoke is rolling up to the sky.

Lily: It's terrible! ______________________________.

Peter: You are right, especially the air pollution.

Lily: ______________________________.

Peter: I want to help out the environment.

Lily: ______________. It's time for us to take some steps to protect our environment.

Peter: Do you have some good ideas?

Lily: ______________________________. And you?

Peter: I'm going to use public transport instead of taking our cars.

Lily: ______________________________.

2. Make up the rest of the dialogue according to the Chinese above.

◈ Culture Corner

雾 霾

雾霾，是雾和霾的组合词。雾霾常见于城市。中国不少地区将雾并入霾一起作为灾害性天气现象进行预警预报，统称为"雾霾天气"。雾霾是特定气候条件与人类活动相互作用的结果。高密度人口的经济及社会活动必然会排放大量细颗粒物（PM 2.5），一旦排放超过大气循环能力和承载度，细颗粒物浓度将持续积聚，此时如果受静稳天气等影响，极易出现大范围的雾霾。

2013 年，雾霾成为年度关键词。这一年的 1 月，共有 4 次雾霾，笼罩过 30 个省，在北京，仅有 5 天不是雾霾天。有报告显示，中国最大的 500 个城市中，只有不到 1% 的城市达到世界卫生组织推荐的空气质量标准，与此同时，世界上污染最严重的 10 个城市有 7 个在中国。

一、主要来源

1. 人为因素

城市有毒颗粒物来源：

第一，汽车尾气。使用柴油的大型车是排放 PM 10 的"重犯"，包括公交车、各单位的班车以及大型运输卡车等。

第二，北方到了冬季烧煤供暖所产生的废气。

第三，工业生产排放的废气。比如，冶金、窑炉与锅炉、机电制造业，还有大量汽修喷漆、建材生产窑炉燃烧排放的废气。

第四，建筑工地和道路交通产生的扬尘。

第五，可生长颗粒，细菌和病毒的粒径相当于 PM 0.1 ~ PM 2.5，空气中的湿度和温度适宜时，微生物会附着在颗粒物上，特别是油烟的颗粒物上，微生物吸收油滴后转化成更多的微生物，使得雾霾中的生物有毒物质生长增多。

第六，家庭装修中也会产生粉尘"雾霾"，室内粉尘弥漫，不仅对工人与用户健康有害，增添清洁负担，粉尘严重时，还给装修工程带来诸多隐患。

2. 气候因素

雾和霾实际上是有区别的。雾是指大气中因悬浮的水汽凝结、能见度低于1千米时的天气现象。灰霾的形成主要是空气中悬浮的大量微粒和气象条件共同作用的结果。

二、主要危害

1. 对人体产生危害

(1) 对呼吸系统的影响

霾的组成成分非常复杂,包括数百种大气化学颗粒物质。其中有害健康的主要是直径小于10微米的气溶胶粒子,它能直接进入并黏附在人体呼吸道和肺泡中。尤其是亚微米粒子会分别沉积于上、下呼吸道和肺泡中,引起急性鼻炎和急性支气管炎等病症。对于支气管哮喘、慢性支气管炎、阻塞性肺气肿和慢性阻塞性肺疾病等慢性呼吸系统疾病患者,雾霾天气可使病情急性发作或急性加重。

(2) 对心血管系统的影响

雾霾天对人体心脑血管疾病的影响也很严重,会阻碍正常的血液循环,导致心血管病、高血压、冠心病、脑溢血,可能诱发心绞痛、心肌梗死、心力衰竭等,使慢性支气管炎出现肺源性心脏病等。

另外,浓雾天气压比较低,人会产生一种烦躁的感觉,血压自然会有所增高。再一方面,雾天往往气温较低,一些高血压、冠心病患者从温暖的室内突然走到寒冷的室外,血管热胀冷缩,也可使血压升高,导致中风、心肌梗死的发生。

(3) 雾霾天气还可导致近地层紫外线的减弱,使空气中的传染性病菌的活性增强,传染病增多。

(4) 不利于儿童成长。由于雾天日照减少,儿童紫外线照射不足,体内维生素D生成不足,对钙的吸收大大减少,严重的会引起婴儿佝偻病,导致儿童生长减慢。

(5) 影响心理健康

专家指出,持续大雾天对人的心理和身体都有影响,从心理上说,大雾天会给人造成沉闷、压抑的感受,会刺激或者加剧心理抑郁的状态。此外,由于雾天光线较弱及导致的低气压,有些人在雾天会产生精神懒散、情绪低落的现象。

(6) 影响生殖能力

有研究表明,长期暴露于高浓度污染的空气中的人群,其精子在体外受精时的成功率可能会降低。研究人员还发现了有毒空气和男性生育能力下降之间的关联 。

(7) 易引发老年痴呆症

2017年2月6日报道,根据一项英国兰卡斯特大学的Maher及其团队发表在《美国国家科学院院刊》上的最新研究发现:"雾霾等空气污染,损伤的不仅是我们的肺,还有我们的大脑。"

2. 对生态环境和交通产生危害

(1) 影响交通安全

雾霾天气时，由于空气质量差、能见度低，容易引起交通阻塞，发生交通事故。在日常行车行走时更应该多观察路况，以免发生危险。

(2) 阴霾天气更易致癌

雾霾天气时光照严重不足，接近底层的紫外线明显减弱，使得空气中细菌很难被杀死，从而传染病的概率大大增加。中国工程院院士、广州呼吸疾病研究所所长钟南山曾在某论坛上指出，近30年来，我国公众吸烟率不断下降，但肺癌患病率上升了4倍多。这可能与雾霾天增加有一定的关系。不但浓雾缠绕、能见度非常低的天气会对人体健康产生影响，时而有雾时而多云的天气也会有同样的问题。

(3) 影响生态环境

雾霾天气对公路、铁路、航空、航运、供电系统、农作物生长等均产生重要影响。雾霾会造成空气质量下降，影响生态环境，给人体健康带来较大危害。

三、预防措施

- 雾霾天气少开窗。
- 外出戴口罩。
- 多喝茶。
- 适量补充维生素D。
- 饮食清淡多喝水。
- 多吃蔬菜。
- 在雾霾天气尽量减少出门。
- 开车注意车速。
- 出门时，做个自我防护，佩戴专门防霾的PM 2.5口罩、防霾鼻罩，过滤PM 2.5，随时随地呼吸新鲜空气。
- 避免雾天锻炼。可以改在太阳出来后再晨练，也可以改为室内锻炼。
- 患者坚持服药。呼吸病患者和心脑血管病患者在雾天更要坚持按时服药。
- 别把窗子关得太严。可以选择中午阳光较充足、污染物较少的时候短时间开窗换气。
- 尽量远离马路。上下班高峰期和晚上大型汽车进入市区这些时间段，污染物浓度最高。
- 补钙、补维生素D，多吃豆腐、雪梨等。

Section 3 Feelings and Moods

Warming-up

1. Match the words with the correct pictures.

A. laugh	B. smile	C. tired	D. confused
E. cry	F. angry	G. sad	H. embarrassed

a. ____________

b. ____________

c. ____________

d. ____________

e. ____________

f. ____________

g. ____________

h. ____________

2. Work in pairs as follows.

A: How are you today?

B: I feel …

Sentence Patterns

Man	Woman
How are you today?	I feel embarrassed.
How do you feel today?	I'm tired.
How have you been recently?	I'm always happy.
I feel very nervous.	Take it easy.
I have been sad.	Cheer up.

Communicating

Dialogue A

(*Mike and Jane are chatting about the exam on the campus.*)

Mike: Hello! How are you today?

Jane: Hi! I feel very nervous. I just had a test and I'm not sure whether I could pass it.

Mike: Take it easy. Now you can't change the exam result.

Jane: That's true. I really should go home and prepare for the next test, but I'm feeling tired.

Mike: Cheer up. Let's go and get a cup of coffee together to relax.

Jane: OK.

Dialogue B

Jane: How have you been recently?

Mike: Well, I'm always happy. If I feel sad, I'll chat with my friends.

Jane: Great idea. I usually just stay at home alone.

Mike: I get bored of it really quickly. I'm always excited about chatting with my close friends.

Jane: I'm too shy. If I meet strangers, I'll feel embarrassed.

Mike: Come on!

Jane: Thank you!

Vocabulary

nervous	[ˈnɜːvəs]	*adj.*	神经的;紧张不安的
tired	[taɪəd]	*adj.*	疲倦的;厌倦的,厌烦的
relax	[rɪˈlæks]	*v.*	放松
recently	[ˈriːsntli]	*adv.*	最近
close	[kləʊz]	*adj.*	亲密的,亲近的
shy	[ʃaɪ]	*adj.*	害羞的;畏缩的,胆怯的
embarrassed	[ɪmˈbærəst]	*adj.*	尴尬的;窘迫的
take it easy			放轻松
cheer up			高兴起来;振作起来
great idea			好主意
get bored of			厌烦的
come on			加油

Practice

1. Finish the following dialogue according to the Chinese.

提示:Mike 遇到 Jane 询问她怎么样。Jane 因考试比较紧张,不确信能否通过考试。Mike 让 Jane 放轻松,考试结果不能被改变。Jane 说她感到很累, Mike 请她一起去喝咖啡,放松一下。Jane 问 Mike 最近如何, Mike 说他总是开心的,如果不开心就找朋友聊聊。Jane 说因为害羞,心情不好时就一个人待在家里。Mike 说如果待在家里,他会很快就厌烦了。最后 Mike 劝 Jane 要加油。

Mike: Hello! ________________________?

Jane: Hi! ________________________.

Mike: Take it easy. ________________________.

Jane: That's true. ________________________.

Mike: Let's go and get a cup of coffee together to relax.

Jane: OK. ________________________?

Mike: Well, ________________________. If I feel depressed, I'll chat with my friends.

Jane: Great idea.

2. Make up the rest of the dialogue according to the Chinese above.

Culture Corner

心情小贴士

一、保持心情愉快的方法

1. 至少要有一种爱好：一个人在生活中要有一些爱好，如旅游、看书等，会使人感到生活充实、满足和愉快。

2. 能尝试新事物：人的生活陷入单调沉闷的“老一套”时，就会感到不愉快，如果去参加一项新的活动，不仅可以扩展生活领域，还会为生活带来新的乐趣。

3. 自己争取多做事：在生活中，如果太依赖他人，对别人的期望太高，就容易失望。若能树立凡能自己做的事，自己去努力做好的观念，则可避免许多由失望带来的痛苦。

4. 交几个知心朋友：友谊有助于身心健康，空闲时与朋友聊聊，既能增长见识，交流信息，又可把自己的烦心事向朋友倾诉，朋友会为你排忧解难，增强自己解决问题的信心和勇气。

5. 不要钻牛角尖：看任何事物都不能认死理，要学会从不同角度去看待事物和分析问题，找出解决问题的不同方法。

6. 学会宽容大度：在生活中，要放宽责备的尺度，善于宽恕和同情他人，处理好人际关系并使之和谐发展。

7. 乐于承认失败与缺陷。

8. 建立合适的期望值。

9. 坚守信念。

10. 乐于接受别人的建议、帮助和忠告。

11. 必须诚实和富于正义感。

12. 要热心帮助别人，给别人以欢乐和幸福。

二、关于心理健康

世界卫生组织将健康定义为：“一个只有在身体健康、心理健康、社会适应良好和道德健康四方面都健全的人，才算完全健康的人。”

1. 心理健康指标：

(1) 了解自我、悦纳自我。

(2) 接受他人，善于与人相处。

(3) 热爱生活，乐于工作和学习。

(4) 适应现实生活。

(5) 能协调与控制情绪。

(6) 人格和谐完整。

(7) 智力正常。

（8）心理行为符合行为特征。

2. 中职生的心理健康特点，主要体现在以下7个方面：

（1）与别人相似。

（2）表现与年龄相符。

（3）善于与人相处。

（4）乐观进取。

（5）适度的反应。

（6）面对现实。

（7）思维合乎逻辑。

3. 学习障碍是一种心理障碍，是一种勤奋学习的腐蚀剂和阻力。给人以方便，就是给自己方便。

4. 中职生的自我心理调节法：

（1）倾诉。

（2）旅游。

（3）读书。

（4）听音乐。

（5）求雅趣。

（6）做好事。

（7）忘却。

5. 在日常生活中，情绪好像是一种很难控制的东西，很可能一件小事就会激起我们很强烈的情绪反应，我们要学会控制它，应做到：

（1）积极参加锻炼和保持良好的膳食习惯。

（2）寻找产生压力的根源。

（3）当面临压力时，学会放松。

（4）拖延转移极端情绪。

（5）适度的宣泄。

6. 新心之语：

（1）我们因助人而快乐，因受助而成长。我们因互助而不再孤单，因自主而实现自我。

（2）如果花开了，就欣赏。如果云开了，就灿烂。如果分开了，就怀念。如果开心了，就珍惜。

（3）送人玫瑰，手有余香；给人快乐，温暖自己。

7. 心情最重要。

你改变不了事实，但可以改变态度。

你改变不了过去，但可以改变现在。

我们不可以控制他人，但可以掌握自己。

我们不可以预知明天，但可以把握今天。

我们不可以样样顺心，但可以事事尽心。
我们不可以左右天气，但可以改变心情。
我们不可以选择容貌，但可以展现笑容。
我们改变不了环境，但可以改变自己。

8. 心理健康的十条标准。

(1) 充分的安全感。
(2) 充分了解自己，并对自己的能力做适当的评估。
(3) 生活的目标切合实际。
(4) 与现实的环境保持接纳。
(5) 能保持人格的完整与和谐。
(6) 具有从经验中学习的能力。
(7) 能保持良好的人际关系。

Section 4 Seeing a Doctor

Warming-up

1. Match the common illnesses with the correct pictures.

A. fever	B. toothache	C. overweight	D. cough
E. headache	F. stomachache	G. backache	H. sneeze

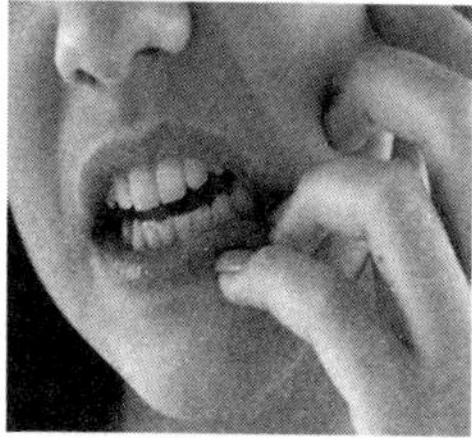

a. ________

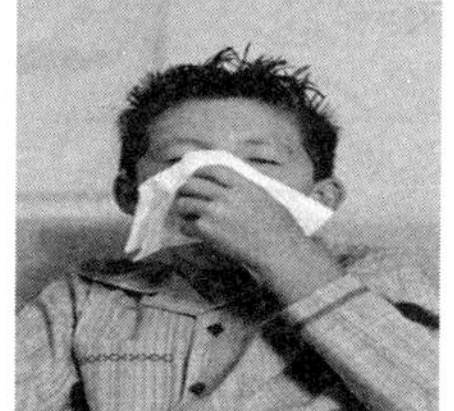

b. ________

c. ________

d. ________

e. ________

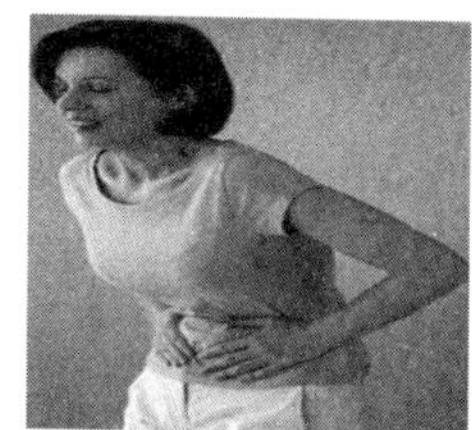

f. ________

g. 

h. ______________

2. *Work in pairs as follows.*

A: What's wrong with you?

B: I've got a …

Sentence Patterns

Doctor	Patient
What's wrong/the matter (with you)?	I don't feel well. /I'm feeling sick.
Did you have anything bad?	I've got a headache/a pain in the …
How long have you been like this?	I feel terrible/bad.
Let me check/look at your …/Take your temperature.	I don't feel like eating anything.
It's not serious. You've got the flu.	Since last night. /About two days.

Communicating

Dialogue A

(*Tom is ill this morning, so he has to go to see a doctor.*)

Tom: Good morning!

Doctor: Good morning! What's the matter?

Tom: I don't feel well, and I've got a headache.

Doctor: How long have you been like that?

Tom: Since last night.

Doctor: OK, let me have a look at your throat. Now open your mouth and say "Ah …"

Tom: Ah …

Dialogue B

Doctor: Oh, your throat is red. But it's not serious. You've got the flu.

Tom: What should I do?

Doctor: Just take some medicine, have a good rest and drink more water.

Tom: How soon can I be all right again?

Doctor: Maybe in three days.

Tom: Thank you!

Doctor: You are welcome!

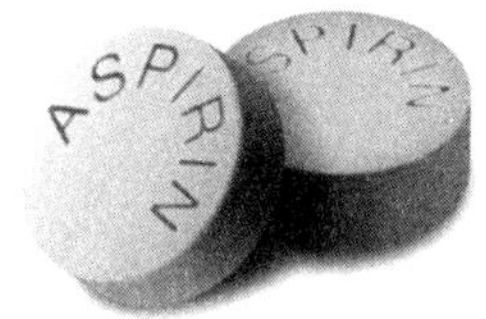

Vocabulary

well	[wel]	*adj.*	健康的
matter	[ˈmætə]	*n.*	问题,毛病;事情,事件;物质
throat	[θrəʊt]	*n.*	咽喉,喉咙
flu	[fluː]	*n.*	流行性感冒,流感
medicine	[ˈmedɪsɪn]	*n.*	药,内服药;医学
have a look			看一看,看一下
take medicine			吃药
have a good rest			好好休息
all right			(病)好了,康复

Practice

1. Finish the following dialogue according to the Chinese.

提示:Jack从晚上起一直肚子疼,他怀疑是不是因为吃不洁的食物,所以第二天上午去看医生。经过检查,医生告诉他不要紧,只是受凉了。他问医生他该怎么做,医生建议他服药,多喝水,休息两天就好了。

Jack: ____________, doctor.

Doctor: Good morning. ____________?

Jack: I've got a pain in my stomach.

Doctor: ____________?

Jack: No. Only some noodles and nothing for breakfast this morning.

Doctor: ____________?

Jack: Since last night.

Doctor: I see. Let me check you.

Jack: Is there anything serious, doctor?

Doctor: ____________. You've just caught a cold.

2. Make up the rest of the dialogue according to the Chinese above.

Culture Corner

世界上医疗体系较好的国家

衡量一个国家的医疗质量并非易事,也很难用一个数字来描述。不过通过将不同国家各项医疗花费对比、打分,即可看出世界上医疗体系较好的几个国家。

1. 墨西哥:医疗服务水平相当,价格却不到美国的一半

每年大量美国人涌入墨西哥接受治疗或去看牙医,这是因为墨西哥医疗服务优质,而价格比美国低。

甚至在墨西哥中等城市,医疗机构都是顶级的。这里的医生通常都在美国、加拿大或者欧洲接受过培训,即使其中一些没有在国外就读医学院,也在国外接受过在职培训。

在墨西哥医疗机构,最新的医疗技术、处方药物等都应有尽有。因严重疾患动大手术或接受医治也不是什么问题。在墨西哥的旅居者可以享受到顶级的医疗服务,总体上价格只有美国的一半不到,而且墨西哥的处方药物价格连美国处方药物价格的一半都不到。

墨西哥合法居民可以从两种医保体系中选择。政府医保体系内的医院和诊所遍布墨西哥全境,大多数旅居者表示,可以在这类医疗机构享受到很好的基本医疗服务,价格也低,每年只有几百美元。

许多旅居者还去私营医疗机构就医,可以通过现金付款或者医保支付。在墨西哥私营医疗机构就医价格也远低于美国,比如,门诊的花费约 30 到 40 美元,检查费用仅为美国的 1/3。

由于墨西哥医疗服务质优价廉,有些美国患者千里迢迢从阿拉斯加州和夏威夷州来到这里求医。墨西卡利位于边境地区,实施特殊的税收制度,是个免税区。这里的药价比边境另一侧低 40% 到 95%。林立的"医疗免税店"吸引着大批美国医疗旅游者。除了美国患者,加拿大人也逐渐加入了墨西哥的医疗旅游的队伍。冬季一到,他们不但可以来到温暖的墨西哥避寒,也可以顺便享受这里性价比极高的医疗服务。

2. 马来西亚:医疗旅游正蓬勃兴起

美元走强、机票价格走低及西方国家医疗开支不断飞涨,这些因素共同推动近年来马来西亚医疗旅游蓬勃兴起。过去五年,赴马来西亚的医疗游客平均增长了 100%。槟城和吉隆坡市是马来西亚两大医疗中心,而且两座城市有多条国际航线通达世界各地。

马来西亚有训练有素的医生,而且其中绝大多数都在美国、澳大利亚以及英国接受过专业培训。此外,在马来西亚就医,等待时间很少甚至完全无须等待。只需在医院进行登记注册,然后等待专家为其看病,中间无须全科医生转诊。

达到国际标准的医疗机构也是消费者赴海外就医的驱动因素之一。槟城和吉隆坡多家医院都通过了著名的 JCI 认证,在东南亚各国属于首批。马来西亚至少有 8 家医院通过了 JCI 认证。此外,马来西亚还有许多优秀的非营利医院。

医疗旅行者赴马来西亚主要是看整形外科、牙科和皮肤科。2016 年,马来西亚共接待了超过 100 多万世界各地的医疗旅游者。

3. 哥伦比亚:重视居民健康福祉

哥伦比亚的医疗保健服务质优价廉。世卫组织(WHO)通过对 191 个国家进行评估,将哥伦比亚的医疗保健体系排在第 22 位,这比加拿大和美国的排名都靠前,这两个国家排名分别为第 30 和第 37。

哥伦比亚全国分布有许多很棒的医院和诊所,能提供不同层级的医疗服务。拉丁美洲 43 家顶级医院中有一半在哥伦比亚(22 家)。在波哥大、麦德林、布卡拉曼加等城市,一些医院已经通过了 JCI 认证。

相比于欧美国家昂贵的医疗费用,在哥伦比亚,同样的手术只需要一半或者更少的费用。麦德林和波哥大的大型医院都拥有世界上最先进、最前沿的医疗设备,有些甚至超过欧美国家的医院。而且语言交流也不是障碍,因为哥伦比亚大中城市的许多医院要么有讲英语的医护人员,要么设有认证的翻译部门。

拥有居住证件并且未满 60 岁旅居者可申请加入政府健康保险 EPS。即使申请者之前就有病史,仍会被接纳进政府保险计划之中,这些疾病的治疗短时间内(6 个月左右)排除在医保范围,但之后会被全额覆盖。

退休者支付的保险费相当于收入的 12%,通常一对夫妇每月需支付保险费 70 美元到 85 美元。公共医疗保险分为三档,其中中档自付费约为 3 美元。自付费主要用于检查、拍 X 光片和处方药物。

60 岁以上的人可选择商业医疗保险作为公共医疗保险的补充。在哥伦比亚,商业保险保费要远低于美国水平。当然保险费高低还取决于所选择的保险公司、保障水平以及申请时的年龄和健康状况。

如果选择不加入医疗保险,自己承担医疗费用,也很容易做到。这里的医疗项目、医院门诊和药物价格等都远低于美国水平。比如,接受专科医生一小时的咨询指导花费约 50 美元。

4. 哥斯达黎加:加入全民医保体系,外国人在公立医院免费看病

作为世界著名医疗旅游目的地,哥斯达黎加以低廉的价格、优质的医疗水平而著称。无论当地人或外国人,均可用低廉的保费参加全民医保体系,在哥斯达黎公立医院接受完全免费的医疗医治。所以吸引不少专为治病而来的游客,比如,来此进行牙科和整容手术。

哥斯达黎加有两种医疗服务体系,来此地的外国人均可享用。

一种被称为"卡哈",是由政府管理运营的全民医保体系,注重提供预防性医疗服务。所有哥斯达黎加公民和合法居民都能享用,包括持有退休签证的外国人。根据居留申请上的收入水平，参保人每月交一定费用，约为收入的6%到12%。缴费后一名申请人及其配偶就能享受医保待遇，一对夫妻平均每月需缴费75美元到150美元。在按月缴纳费用后，一个人的医疗服务需求基本上都能得到满足，如看医生门诊（包括专家门诊）、诊断检查、开具处方药、外科手术等，而且不存在因年龄或既有疾病被排除在外的情况。虽然还存在门诊等候时间长等问题，但是大多数旅居者表示，"卡哈"提供了很好的医疗服务。

另一种是私营医疗服务体系。哥斯达黎加有一个大规模私营医疗系统，医生、诊所和医院遍布全国。消费者在这些私营医院看病可支付现金，医生门诊50美元，专家门诊80美元到100美元，超声检查波检查75美元，甚至大型手术也很价廉，价格只相当于美国的一半。

旅居者还可以享用医疗保险，国际保险公司和哥斯达黎加公司提供的医保都可供选择。大多数私营医院都设有专门的部门，来帮助国外病人处理保险支付事宜。

通常，旅居者会私营和公立医疗服务搭配使用。他们或许会掏钱去私立医院看病，然后在"卡哈"体系内的药房免费拿处方药。或者如果在公立医院耗时过长，他们就会去私营医院看病。

需要注意的是，尽管哥斯达黎加各地都有不错的医院，但是最好的医院和大多数专科医生集中在首都圣何塞。因此如果得了重病，很可能需要前往圣何塞就医。

Module 7

B What U Wanna B

B What U Wanna B

doctor, actor, lawyer or a singer 医生，演员，律师，还是歌手？

why not president, be a dreamer 为什么不能是当总统呢，要成为一个梦想家

you can be just the one you wanna be 只要你想，你就能成为你想做的人

policeman, fire fighter or a postman 警察，消防队员，或者是邮递员

why not something like your old man 为什么不能是像你父亲之类的人呢？

you can be just the one you wanna be 只要你想，你就能成为你想做的人

doctor, actor, lawyer or a singer 医生，演员，律师，还是歌手？

why not president, be a dreamer 为什么不能是当总统呢，要成为一个梦想家

you can be just the one you wanna be 只要你想，你就能成为你想做的人

I know that we all got one thing 我知道我们都有一样东西

that we all share together 我们都拥有的

we got that one nice dream 我们都有一个美好的梦想

we live for 我们为之存在

you never know what life could bring 你永远不会知道生活会带来什么

coz nothing last for ever 因为没有什么东西能永恒存在

just hold on to the team you play for 只要在你的团队中坚持扮演好你自己的角色

I know you could reach the top 我知道你是最棒的

make sure that you won't stop 确保你不会停下

be the one that you wanna be 成为你想成为的人

now sing this with me 现在和我一起唱吧

doctor, actor, lawyer or a singer 医生，演员，律师，还是歌手？

why not president, be a dreamer 为什么不能是当总统呢，要成为一个梦想家

you can be just the one you wanna be 只要你想，你就能成为你想做的人

policeman, fire fighter or a postman 警察，消防队员，或者是邮递员

why not something like your old man 为什么不能是像你父亲之类的人呢?
you can be just the one you wanna be 只要你想，你就能成为你想做的人
we may have different ways to think 我们也许有不同的思考方式
but it doesn't really matter 但是真的不要紧
we all caught up in the steam of this life 我们都赶上了这趟人生之旅
focus on every little thing 留意每一样平凡的东西
that's what does really matter 那才是我们真正在意的
luxury cars and bling 奢华的车和物质
that's not real life 那不是真正的生活
I know you could reach the top 我知道你是最棒的
make sure that you won't stop 确保你不会停下
be the one that you wanna be 成为你想成为的人
now sing this with me 现在和我一起唱吧
doctor, actor, lawyer or a singer 医生，演员，律师，还是歌手?
why not president, be a dreamer 为什么不能是当总统呢，要成为一个梦想家

Section 1 Job Interviews

Warming-up

1. Match the words or phrases with the correct pictures.

A. resume	B. interview	C. diploma	D. graduation
E. application letter	F. credential	G. confidence	H. interview attire

a. ________________

b. ________________

c. ________________

d. ______________ e. ______________ f. ______________

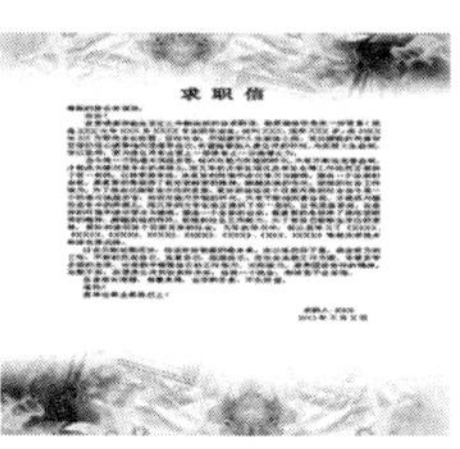

求职信

g. ______________ h. ______________

2. ***Work in pairs as follows.***

A: I will go to a company for an interview tomorrow. Could you tell me what I should prepare?

B: Well, you should have something ready, such as ...

A: Anything else?

B: It is also very important to ... during the interview.

Sentence Patterns

Interviewer	Interviewee
What kind of job do you want? Can you work under pressure? What would you like to achieve in life? You'll be hearing from us next week. I'm sorry to say I can't offer you the job.	I want to find a job which is related to my major. Yes, I find it stimulating. My long-range career is to be the best technician in this field. When will you let me know the result? That's all right. Thank you very much for your advice. I can try other places.

Communicating

Dialogue A

(*Liu Gang is the manager of Human Resources of Shanghai Volkswagen. He is now in need of a vehicle maintenance technician. Wang Hai wants to get this job. So he goes there to apply for the job.*)

Liu Gang: Good morning, can I help you?

Wang Hai: Good morning, I'd like some information about a job opening for the position of a vehicle maintenance technician in your company. Is it still available?

Liu Gang: Yes. Do you have your resume and necessary credentials with you?

Wang Hai: Yes, here they are.

Liu Gang: Just leave them here and we'll get in touch with you for the job interview.

Dialogue B

Liu Gang: Welcome to Shanghai Volkswagen!

Wang Hai: Nice to meet you!

Liu Gang: Would you like to introduce yourself?

Wang Hai: Well, I'm going to graduate from Yizheng Technician College next July. My major is Vehicle Maintenance. I am a hard-working, helpful and confident student.

Liu Gang: What did you study at school?

Wang Hai: I studied English, Chinese, Maths, Engine Mechanics, etc.

Liu Gang: What skills do you have?

Wang Hai: I can diagnose the general trouble with automobile and repair common troubles of them.

Liu Gang: OK. Thank you for coming to our interview. We will call you as soon as possible.

Wang Hai: Thank you very much, Mr. Liu. I'll look forward to hearing from you. Goodbye.

Vocabulary

position	[pə'zɪʃn]	*n.*	职位,位置
available	[ə'veɪləbl]	*adj.*	可获得的
resume	[rɪ'zjuːm]	*n.*	简历,履历
credential	[krə'denʃl]	*n.*	证件,文凭
graduate	['grædʒuət]	*v.*	毕业
confident	['kɒnfɪdənt]	*adj.*	有信心的
diagnose	['daɪəgnəuz]	*vt.*	诊断
HR(Human Resource)			人力资源
Shanghai Volkswagen			上海大众
vehicle maintenance technician			汽车维修技师
apply for			申请
get in touch with			与……取得联系
graduate from			从……毕业

Practice

1. *Choose the best answer from the box to complete the dialogue.*

A. All right.
B. What were your responsibilities there?
C. I don't think there will be any problem.
D. I live with two women, my cousin and one of her students.
E. Well, it's hard to make a living as a musician.

Interviewer: Mr. Wang, could you tell me why you're applying for a job in an office?
Interviewee: ____________
Interviewer: I know. But I think that your music may interfere with (干扰) your responsibilities in the office.
Interviewee: ____________ This job doesn't start until 10 a.m. , right?
Interviewer: Yes. Well, your last job was in a doctor's office.
Interviewee: Right.
Interviewer: ____________
Interviewee: I had to answer the phones, and make appointments.
Interviewer: I see. Now the only thing is that you'd be the only man working in an office full of women.
Interviewee: ____________ It's no big deal to me.
Interviewer: OK, you'll be hearing from us in a day or two.
Interviewee: ____________ Thanks for your time.

2. *Finish the following dialogue according to the Chinese.*

提示:魏华正在接受怀特先生的面试。怀特先生问她是否确定申请经理助理(assistant manager)一职。得到魏华的肯定回答后,怀特先生先后询问了魏华所学专业以及如果给她提供这份工作,她是否能做好准备。魏华问何时能开始工作,怀特先生说会电话通知她。

Mr White: Come in, and take a seat, please.
Wei Hua: Thank you, sir.
Mr White: You're Wei Hua, ____________?
Wei Hua: Yes, I am.
Mr White: __________ when you were in university?
Wei Hua: I majored in Business Management(商业管理).
Mr White: I see. Are you prepared to do a probationary(试用的) year ____________?
Wei Hua: Yes. ________________________?

Mr White: ________________________ if we decide to hire you.

Wei Hua: Goodbye. Thank you very much for your interview.

Culture Corner

(一) 求职面试中的中西方文化差异

1. 行为的差异

东方文化中,与人谈话时一般不直视对方时间太久。尤其是在与职位和年龄比自己要高的人交谈时,一般不直视,以示尊敬。

而在西方文化中,最基本的交谈礼仪就是尽量直视对方的眼睛,不东张西望。这一点是中国学生容易忽略的细节。尤其在西方,谈话人眼睛长久凝视地面会给人一种不可靠、似乎在遮掩什么的感觉。

2. 表达方式的差异

东方文化往往让人表现的谦逊好学,所以很多同学面试时比较被动,回答问题时往往用简单的 Yes 或 No,担心说得多了,给人的印象不好。

其实在英国公司面试的时候,简短的陈述是很必要的。除了非常简单的问题,一般来说,考生对每个问题的回答最好用三到五句话。在面试官要求描述一个经历或事件的时候,可以适当延长回答。但也要注意不要长篇大论,描述太多细节而没有突出要点。

二、 价值观念的差异

东方的价值观念中,面试回答如:"我刚毕业,没有什么社会经验。如果能给我一个锻炼的机会,我非常感激。至于工资多少,我并不在意。"可能是雇主爱听的回答。

而在西方逻辑中,公司聘人希望发现能胜任职位要求的人,而不是一个对工作职位毫无要求的人。

(二) 求职面试时常被问到的问题与技巧性回答

1. 请你自我介绍一下你自己。

回答提示:一般人回答这个问题过于平常,只说姓名、年龄、爱好、工作经验,这些在简历上都有。其实企业最希望知道的是求职者能否胜任工作,包括:最强的技能、最深入研究的知识领域、个性中最积极的部分、做过的最成功的事、主要的成就等,要突出积极的个性和做事的能力,说得合情合理。企业很重视一个人的礼貌,求职者要尊重考官,在回答每个问题之后都说一句"谢谢",企业喜欢有礼貌的求职者。

2. 你觉得你个性上最大的优点是什么?

回答提示:沉着冷静、条理清楚、立场坚定、乐于助人和关心他人、适应能力强、幽默感、乐观和友爱。我在 XX 经过一到两年的培训及项目实战,加上实习工作,使我适合这份工作。

3. 说说你最大的缺点。

回答提示:这个问题企业问的概率很大,通常不希望听到直接回答缺点是什么,如果求职者说自己小心眼、爱忌妒人、非常懒、脾气大、工作效率低,企业肯定不会录用你。绝对不要自作聪明地回答“我最大的缺点是过于追求完美”,有的人以为这样回答会显得自己比较出色,但事实上不是。企业喜欢求职者从自己的优点说起,中间加一些小缺点,最后再把问题转回到优点上,突出优点的部分,企业喜欢聪明的求职者。

4. 你对加班的看法?

回答提示:实际上好多公司问这个问题,并不证明一定要加班,只是想测试你是否愿意为公司奉献。

回答样本:如果是工作需要,我会义不容辞加班,我现在单身,没有任何家庭负担,可以全身心地投入工作。但同时我也会提高工作效率,减少不必要的加班。

5. 你对薪资的要求?

回答提示:如果你对薪酬的要求太低,那显然贬低自己的能力;如果你对薪酬的要求太高,那又会显得你要求过重,公司受用不起。一些雇主通常都事先对招聘的职位定下开支预算,因而他们第一次提出的价钱往往是他们所能给予的最高价钱,他们问你只不过想证实一下这笔钱是否足以引起你对该工作的兴趣。

回答样本一:我对工资没有硬性要求,我相信贵公司在处理我的问题上会友善合理。我注重的是找对工作机会,所以只要条件公平,我不会计较太多。

回答样本二:我受过系统的软件编程的训练,不需要进行大量的培训,而且我本人也对编程特别感兴趣。因此,我希望公司能根据我的情况和市场标准的水平,给我合理的薪水。

6. 在五年的时间内,你的职业规划?

回答提示:这是每个应聘者都不希望被问到的问题,但是几乎每个人都会被问道,比较多的答案是“管理者”。但是近几年来,许多公司都已经建立了专门的技术途径。这些工作地位往往被称作“顾问”“参议技师”或“高级软件工程师”等。当然,说出其他一些你感兴趣的职位也是可以的,比如,产品销售部经理、生产部经理等一些与你的专业有相关背景的工作。要知道,面试官总是喜欢有进取心的应聘者,此时如果说“不知道”,或许就会使你丧失一个好机会。最普通的回答应该是“我准备在技术领域有所作为”或“我希望能按照公司的管理思路发展”。

7. 你朋友对你的评价?

回答提示: 想从侧面了解一下你的性格及与人相处的问题。

回答样本一:我的朋友都说我是一个可以信赖的人。因为我一旦答应别人的事情,就一定会做到。如果我做不到,就不会轻易许诺。

回答样本二:我觉得我是一个比较随和的人,与不同的人都可以友好相处。在我与人相处时,我总是能站在别人的角度考虑问题。

8. 你还有什么问题要问吗?

回答提示:企业的这个问题看上去可有可无,其实很关键,企业不喜欢说“没问题”的人,因为注重员工的个性和创新能力。如果有人这样问:贵公司对新入公司的员工有没有什么培训项目,我可以参加吗?或者说贵公司的晋升机制是什么样的?企业将很欢迎,因为体现出你对学习的热情和对公司的忠诚度以及你的上进心。

9. 如果通过这次面试我们单位录用了你，但工作一段时间却发现你根本不适合这个职位，你怎么办？

回答提示：一段时间发现工作不适合我，有两种情况：① 如果确实热爱这个职业，那就要不断学习，虚心向领导和同事学习业务知识和处事经验，了解这个职业的精神内涵和职业要求，力争减少差距。② 如果觉得这个职业可有可无，那还是趁早换个职业，去发现适合我的职业，这样对单位和我个人都有好处。

10. 在完成某项工作时，你认为领导要求的方式不是最好的，自己还有更好的方法，你应该怎么做？

回答提示：① 原则上我会尊重和服从领导的工作安排，同时私底下找机会以请教的口吻，婉转地表达自己的想法，看看领导是否能改变想法。② 如果领导没有采纳我的建议，我也同样会按领导的要求认真地去完成这项工作。③ 还有一种情况，假如领导的要求违背原则，我会坚决提出反对意见，如领导仍固执己见，我会毫不犹豫地再向上级领导反映。

11. 如果你的工作出现失误，给本公司造成经济损失，你认为该怎么办？

回答提示：① 我本意是为公司努力工作，如果造成经济损失，我认为首要的问题是想方设法去弥补或挽回经济损失。如果我无能力负责，希望单位帮助解决。② 分清责任，各负其责，如果是我的责任，我甘愿受罚；如果是一个我负责的团队中成员的失误，也不能幸灾乐祸，作为一个团队，需要互相提携共同完成工作，安慰同事并且帮助同事查找原因总结经验。③ 总结经验教训，一个人的一生不可能不犯错误，重要的是能从自己的或者是别人的错误中吸取经验教训，并在今后的工作中避免发生同类的错误。检讨自己的工作方法，分析问题的深度和力度是否不够，以致出现了本可以避免的错误。

12. 如果你做的一项工作受到上级领导的表扬，但你主管领导却说是他做的，你该怎样？

回答提示：我首先不会找那位上级领导说明这件事，我会主动找我的主管领导来沟通，因为沟通是解决人际关系的最好办法，但结果会有两种：① 我的主管领导认识到自己的错误，我想我会视具体情况决定是否原谅他。② 他变本加厉地来威胁我，那我会毫不犹豫地找我的上级领导反映此事，因为他这样做会造成负面影响，对今后的工作不利。

13. 谈谈你对跳槽的看法？

回答提示：① 正常的“跳槽”能促进人才合理流动，应该支持。② 频繁的跳槽对单位和个人双方都不利，应该反对。

14. 工作中你难以和同事、上司相处，你该怎么办？

回答提示：① 我会服从领导的指挥，配合同事的工作。② 我会从自身找原因，仔细分析是不是自己工作做得不好让领导不满意，同事看不惯。还要看看是不是为人处世方面做得不好，如果是这样的话，我会努力改正。③ 如果我找不到原因，我会找机会跟他们沟通，请他们指出我的不足，有问题就及时改正。④ 作为优秀的员工，应该时刻以大局为重，即使在一段时间内，领导和同事对我不理解，我也会做好本职工作，虚心向他们学习，我相信，他们会看见我在努力,总有一天会对我微笑的。

15. 假设你在某单位工作,成绩比较突出,得到领导的肯定。但同时你发现同事们越来越孤立你,你怎么看这个问题?你准备怎么办?

回答提示:① 成绩比较突出,得到领导的肯定是件好事情,以后更加努力。② 检讨一下自己是不是对工作的热心度超过同事间交往的热心了,加强同事间的交往及培养共同的兴趣爱好。③ 工作中,切勿伤害别人的自尊心。④ 不在领导前拨弄是非。

16. 你对于我们公司了解多少?

回答提示:在去公司面试前上网查一下该公司主营业务。如回答:贵公司有意改变策略,加强与国外大厂的 OEM 合作,自有品牌的部分则透过海外经销商。

17. 请说出你选择这份工作的动机。

回答提示:这是想知道面试者对这份工作的热忱度及理解度,并筛选因一时兴起而来应试的人,如果是无经验者,可以强调"就算职种不同,也希望有机会发挥之前的经验"。

18. 你最擅长的技术方向是什么?

回答提示:说和你要应聘的职位相关的课程,表现一下自己的热忱没有什么坏处。

19. 你能为我们公司带来什么呢?

回答提示:① 假如你可以的话,试着告诉他们你可以减低他们的费用——"我已经接受过 XX 近两年专业的培训,立刻就可以上岗工作"。② 企业很想知道未来的员工能为企业做什么,求职者应再次重述自己的优势,然后说:"就我的能力,我可以做一个优秀的员工,在组织中发挥能力,给组织带来高效率和更多的收益。"企业喜欢求职者就申请的职位表明自己的能力,比如申请营销之类的职位,可以说:"我可以开发大量的新客户,同时,对老客户做更全面、更周到的服务,开发老客户的新需求。"

20. 你的业余爱好是什么?

回答提示:找一些富于团体合作精神的爱好。这里有一个真实的故事:有人被否决掉,因为他的爱好是深海潜水。主考官说:因为这是一项单人活动,我不敢肯定他能否适应团体工作。

21. 作为被面试者给我打一下分。

回答提示:试着列出四个优点和一个非常小的缺点(可以抱怨一下设施,没有明确责任人的缺点是不会有人介意的)。

22. 你怎么理解你应聘的职位?

回答提示:把岗位职责和任务及工作态度阐述一下。

23. 喜欢这份工作的哪一点?

回答提示:每个人的价值观不同,自然评价的标准也会不同,但是在回答面试官这个问题时可不能太直接就把自己心里的话说出来,尤其是薪资方面的问题,一些无伤大雅的回答是不错的考虑,如交通方便、工作性质及内容颇能符合自己的兴趣等都是不错的答案。如果这时自己能仔细思考出这份工作的与众不同之处,相信在面试上会大大加分。

24. 为什么要离职?

回答提示:① 回答这个问题时一定要小心,就算在前一个工作中受到再大的委屈,对公司有多少的怨言,都千万不要表现出来,尤其要避免对公司本身主管的批评,避免给面试官带来负面情绪及留下负面印象。建议此时最好的回答方式是将问题归咎在自己身上,例如,觉得工作没有学习发展的空间,自己想在新的工作单位多加学习,或是前一份工作与自己的职业生涯规划不一致等,回答的答案最好是积极正面的。② 我希望获得一份更好的工作,如果机会来临,我会抓住。

25. 说说你对行业、技术发展趋势的看法。

回答提示:企业对这个问题很感兴趣,只有有备而来的求职者能够过关。求职者可以直接在网上查找对你所申请的行业部门的信息,只有深入了解才能产生独特的见解。企业认为最聪明的求职者对所面试的公司预先了解很多,包括公司各个部门发展情况,在面试回答问题的时候可以提到所了解的情况。

26. 对工作的期望与目标何在?

回答提示:这是面试者用来评价求职者是否对自己有一定程度的期望、对这份工作是否了解的问题。对工作有明确学习目标的人通常学习较快,对于新工作自然较容易进入状态,这时建议你最好针对工作的性质进行阐述,如业务员的工作可以这样回答:"我的目标是能成为一个超级业务员,将公司的产品推销出去,取得最好的业绩;为了达到这个目标,我一定会努力学习,而我相信以我认真负责的态度,一定可以实现这个目标。"其他类似的工作也可以比照这个方式来回答,只要在目标方面稍微修改一下就可以了。

27. 说说你的家庭。

回答提示:企业面试时询问家庭问题不是非要知道求职者家庭的情况,企业不喜欢探究个人隐私,而是要了解家庭背景对求职者的塑造和影响。企业希望听到的重点也在于家庭对求职者的积极影响。企业最喜欢听到的是:我很爱我的家庭,我的家庭一向很和睦,虽然我的父亲和母亲都是普通人,但是从小我就看到我父亲起早贪黑,每天工作特别勤劳,他的行动无形中培养了我认真负责的态度和勤劳的精神。我母亲为人善良,对人热情,特别乐于助人,所以在单位人缘很好,她的一言一行也一直在教导我做人的道理。企业相信和睦的家庭关系对一个人的成长有潜移默化的影响。

28. 就你申请的这个职位,你认为你还欠缺什么?

回答提示:企业喜欢问求职者弱点,但精明的求职者一般不直接回答。他们希望看到求职者继续重复自己的优势,然后说:"就这个职位和我的能力来说,我相信自己是可以胜任的,只是缺乏经验,这个问题我想我可以进入公司以后以最短的时间来解决,我的学习能力很强,我相信可以很快融入公司的企业文化,进入工作状态。"

29. 你欣赏哪种性格的人?

回答提示:诚实、不死板且容易相处的人,有"实际行动"的人。

30. 你通常如何处理别人的批评?

回答提示:① 沉默是金,不必说什么,否则情况更糟,不过我会接受建议性的批评。

② 我会等大家冷静下来再讨论。

31．怎样对待自己的失败？

回答提示：我们大家生来都不是十全十美的，有失败很正常。

32．你为什么愿意到我们公司来工作？

回答提示：对于这个问题，你要格外小心，如果你已经对该单位做了研究，你可以回答，像“公司本身的高技术开发环境很吸引我”“我希望能够进入一家能共同成长的公司”“你们公司一直都稳定发展，在近几年来在市场上很有竞争力”“我认为贵公司能够给我提供一个与众不同的发展道路”，这都显示出你已经做了一些调查，也说明你对自己的未来有了较为具体的远景规划。

33．你和别人发生过争执吗？你是怎样解决的？

回答提示：这是面试中最险恶的问题，其实是面试官设下的一个陷阱，千万不要说任何人的过错，应知成功解决矛盾是一个协作团体中成员所必备的能力。假如你在一个服务行业工作，这个问题是最重要的一个环节。你是否能获得这份工作，取决于这个问题的回答。他们通过这个问题了解你的成熟度和处世能力。

34．新到一个部门，一天一个客户来找你解决问题，你努力想解决问题，让他满意，可是始终不行，他投诉你们部门工作效率低，你这个时候怎么作？

回答提示：①首先，我会保持冷静。作为一名工作人员，在工作中遇到各种各样的问题是正常的，关键是如何认识它，积极应对，妥善处理。②其次，我会反思一下客户不满意的原因。一是看是否自己在解决问题上的确有考虑的不周到的地方；二是看是否客户不太了解相关的服务规定而提出超出规定的要求；三是看是否客户了解相关的规定，但是提出的要求不合理。③再次，根据原因采取相应的对策。如果是自己确有不周到的地方，按照服务规定做出合理的安排，并向客户做出解释；如果是客户不太了解政策规定而造成的误解，我会向他做出进一步的解释，消除他的误会；如果是客户提出的要求不符合政策规定，我会明确地向他指出。④最后，我会把整个事情的处理情况向领导做出说明，希望得到他的理解和支持。我不会因为客户投诉了我而丧失工作的热情和积极性，会一如既往地牢记为客户服务的宗旨，争取早日做一名领导信任、公司放心、客户满意的职员。

35．对这项工作你有哪些可预见的困难？

回答提示：① 不宜直接说出具体的困难，否则可能令对方怀疑应聘者能力不行。② 可以尝试迂回战术，说出应聘者对困难所持有的态度——工作中出现一些困难是正常的，也是难免的，但是只要有坚忍不拔的毅力、良好的合作精神以及事前周密而充分的准备，任何困难都是可以克服的。

36．如果我录用你，你将怎样开展工作？

回答提示：① 如果应聘者对于应聘的职位缺乏足够的了解，最好不要直接说出自己开展工作的具体办法。② 可以尝试采用迂回战术来回答，如：首先听取领导的指示和要求，然后就有关情况进行了解和熟悉，接下来制订一份近期的工作计划并报领导批准，最后根据计划开展工作。

37. 你希望与什么样的上级共事?

回答提示:① 通过应聘者对上级的“希望”可以判断出应聘者对自我要求的意识,这既是一个陷阱,又是一次机会。② 最好回避对上级具体的希望,多谈对自己的要求。③ 如,作为刚步入社会的新人,我应该多要求自己尽快熟悉环境、适应环境,而不应该对环境提出什么要求,只要能发挥我的专长就可以了。

38. 与上级意见不一致,你将怎么办?

回答提示:① 一般可以这样回答:“我会给上级以必要的解释和提醒,在这种情况下,我会服从上级的意见。”② 如果面试你的是总经理,而你所应聘的职位另有一位经理,且这位经理当时不在场,可以这样回答:“对于非原则性问题,我会服从上级的意见,对于涉及公司利益的重大问题,我希望能向更高层领导反映。”

39. 你工作经验欠缺,如何能胜任这项工作?

常规思路:① 如果招聘单位对应届毕业生的应聘者提出这个问题,说明招聘公司并不真正在乎“经验”,关键看应聘者怎样回答。② 对这个问题的回答最好要体现出应聘者的诚恳、机智、果敢及敬业。③ 如:作为应届毕业生,在工作经验方面的确会有所欠缺,因此在读书期间我一直利用各种机会在这个行业里做兼职。我也发现,实际工作远比书本知识丰富、复杂。我有较强的责任心、适应能力和学习能力,而且比较勤奋,所以在兼职中均能圆满完成各项工作,从中获取的经验也令我受益匪浅。请贵公司放心,学校所学及兼职的工作经验使我一定能胜任这个职位。

40. 如果你在这次面试中没有被录用,你怎么打算?

回答提示:现在的社会是一个竞争的社会,从这次面试中也可看出这一点,有竞争就必然有优劣,有成功必定就会有失败。往往成功的背后有许多的困难和挫折,如果这次失败了也仅仅是一次而已,只有经过经验经历的积累才能塑造出一个成功者。我会从以下几个方面来正确看待这次失败:① 要敢于面对,面对这次失败不气馁,接受现实。要有自信,相信自己经历了这次之后经过努力一定能行,能够超越自我。② 善于反思,对于这次面试经验要认真总结,思考剖析,能够从自身的角度找差距。正确对待自己,实事求是地评价自己,辩证地看待自己的长短得失,做一个明白人。③ 走出阴影,要克服这一次失败带给自己的心理压力,时刻牢记自己弱点,防患于未然,加强学习,提高自身素质。

41. 假如你晚上要去送一个出国的同学去机场,可单位临时有事非你办不可,你怎么办?

回答提示:我觉得工作是第一位的,但朋友间的情谊也是不能偏废的,这个问题我觉得要按照当时具体的情况来决定。① 如果我的朋友晚上 9 点钟的飞机,而我的加班 8 点就能够完成的话,那就最理想了,干完工作去机场,皆大欢喜。② 如果说工作不是很紧急,加班仅仅是为了明天上班的时候能把报告交到办公室,那完全可以跟领导打声招呼,先去机场然后回来加班,晚点睡就是了。③ 如果工作很紧急,两者不可能兼顾的情况下,我觉得可以有两种选择:如果不是全单位都加班的话,是不是可以要其他同事来代替一下工作,自己去机场,哪怕就是代替你离开的那一会儿;如果连这一点都做不到的话,那只好打电话给朋友解释一下,相信他会理解,毕竟工作做完了就完了,朋友还是可以再见面的。

42. 谈谈你过去的工作经验中,最令你挫折的事情?

回答提示:曾经接触过一个客户,原本就有耳闻他们以挑剔出名,所以事前的准备工夫做得十分充分,也投入了相当多的时间与精力,最后客户虽然没有照单全收,但是接受的程度已经出乎我们意料了。原以为从此可以合作愉快,却得知客户最后因为预算关系选择了另一家代理商,之前的努力因而付诸流水。尽管如此,我还是从这次的经验中学到很多,如对该产业的了解,整个团队的默契也更好了。

分析:借此了解你对挫折的容忍度及调解方式。

43. 如何安排自己的时间? 会不会排斥加班?

回答提示:基本上,如果上班工作有效率,工作量合理的话,应该不太需要加班。可是我也知道有时候难免加班,加上现在工作都采用责任制,所以我会调配自己的时间,全力配合。

44. 为什么我们要在众多的面试者中选择你?

回答提示:根据我对贵公司的了解以及我在这份工作上所累积的专业、经验及人脉,相信正是贵公司所找寻的人才。而我在工作态度、EQ 上,也有成熟的一面,和主管、同事都能合作愉快。

45. 你在学校属于好学生吗?

回答提示:企业的招聘者很精明,问这个问题可以试探出很多问题:如果求职者学习成绩好,就会说:是的,我的成绩很好,所有的成绩都很优异。当然,判断一个学生是不是好学生有很多标准,在学校期间我认为成绩是重要的,其他方面包括思想道德、实践经验、团队精神、沟通能力也都是很重要的,我在这些方面也做得很好,应该说我是一个全面发展的学生。如果求职者成绩不尽理想,便会说:我认为一个好学生的标准是多元化的,我的学习成绩还可以,在其他方面我的表现也很突出,比如,我去很多地方实习过,我很喜欢在快节奏和压力下工作,我在学生会组织过××活动,锻炼了我的团队合作精神和组织能力。有经验的招聘者一听就会明白,企业喜欢诚实的求职者。

46. 谈谈如何适应办公室工作的新环境。

回答提示:① 办公室里每个人有各自的岗位与职责,不得擅离岗位。② 根据领导指示和工作安排,制订工作计划,提前预备,并按计划完成。③ 多请示并及时汇报,遇到不明白的要虚心请教。④ 抓间隙时间,多学习,努力提高自己的业务水平。

47. 工作中学习到了些什么?

回答提示:这是针对跳槽者提出的问题,建议此时可以配合面试工作的特点作为主要依据来回答,如业务工作需要与人沟通,便可举出之前工作与人沟通的例子,经历了哪些困难,学习到哪些经验,把握这些要点做陈述,就可以轻易过关了。

48. 何时可以到职?

回答提示:大多数企业会关心就职时间,最好是回答"如果被录用的话,到职日可按公司规定上班",但如果还未辞去上一个工作,上班时间又太近,似乎有些强人所难,因为交接至少要一个月的时间，应进一步说明原因，录取公司应该会通融的。

49. 你并非毕业于名牌院校？

回答提示：是否毕业于名牌院校不重要，重要的是有能力完成您交给我的工作，我接受了 XX 的职业培训，掌握的技能完全可以胜任贵公司现在的工作，而且我比一些名牌院校的应届毕业生的动手能力还要强，我想我更适合贵公司这个职位。

Section 2 Asking for Leave

Warming-up

1. Match the words or phrases with the correct pictures.

A. visiting the sick	B. travelling	C. cough	D. traffic jam
E. attending a training	F. fracture	G. wedding	H. going on a business trip

a. ________________

b. ________________

c. ________________

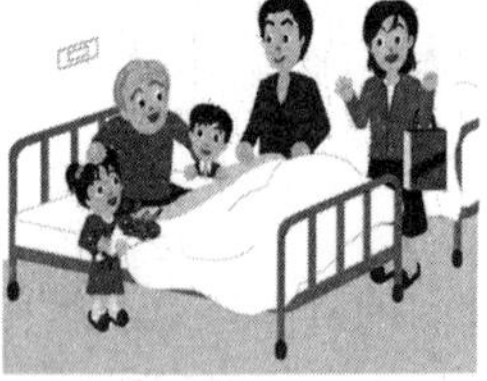

d. ________________

e. ________________

f. ________________

g. ________________

h. ________________

2. Work in pairs as follows.

A: Could I have one day off tomorrow?

B: Well, what's wrong with you?

A: …

B: OK, no problem.

Sentence Patterns

A	B
Could I have one day off tomorrow?	No problem. /I'm afraid not.
What's wrong with you?	I've got a headache/a pain in the …
I'm not feeling well. I'll ask for a day's leave to see the doctor.	No problem. I hope you'll get better soon.
I want to ask for leave for a week.	Why? What happened?
Fill in an absence form, and I will sign it.	Thank you very much.

Communicating

Dialogue A

(*Liu Tao is not feeling well. He will ask for a day's leave to see the doctor.*)

Liu Tao: I am sorry, but I cannot stay for the rest of class today.

Li Ming: Why? What happened?

Liu Tao: I'm not feeling well.

Li Ming: What's wrong with you?

Liu Tao: I feel as if I am going to be sick.

Li Ming: Well, you'd better telephone our teacher and ask for a day's leave to see the doctor.

Liu Tao: I know and I'll call him later.

Li Ming: I hope that you are feeling better soon. Call me if you have any questions.

Dialogue B

(*Wang Hui's best friend will get married tomorrow. She is asking for a day's leave now.*)

Wang Hui: Excuse me, may I ask a day off?

Boss: For what?

Wang Hui: My best friend will get married tomorrow.

Boss: I see. Are you the bridesmaid?

Wang Hui: Yes, I am one of them.

Boss: OK, you can have tomorrow off.

Wang Hui: Thank you, sir!

Boss: Oh, I forgot to tell you there will be an important meeting tomorrow.

Wang Hui: Oh! What shall I do? I have promised her to attend her wedding.

Boss: Well, you can find someone to attend the meeting for you.

Wang Hui: Thank you so much!

Boss: It's my pleasure. Hope you enjoy the wedding!

Vocabulary

sick	[sɪk]	*adj.*	不舒服的,生病的
happen	[ˈhæp(ə)n]	*vi.*	发生
bridesmaid	[ˈbraɪdzmeɪd]	*n.*	伴娘
promise	[ˈprɒmɪs]	*vt.*	允诺,许诺
attend	[əˈtend]	*vt.*	出席,参加
wedding	[ˈwedɪŋ]	*n.*	婚礼,婚宴
ask for leave			请假
as if			好像,似乎
get married			结婚

Practice

1. Choose the best answer from the box to complete the dialogue.

A. Did you see the doctor?	B. Are you feeling better now?
C. Was it serious?	D. What was wrong with you?
E. What did the doctor say?	

A: Hi, Li Jun. You were not at school yesterday. ____________

B: Oh, I had a headache and I had to ask for a sick leave.

A: Sorry to hear that. ____________

B: Yes, my mother took me to the hospital.

A: ____________

B: The doctor checked me over and said I had a cold.

A: ____________

B: Yes, a little. The doctor told me to take the medicine three times a day and have plenty of water.

A: ____________

B: Yes, much better. But I've missed so many lessons.

A: Don't worry about it. I'll help you later.

B: Thanks a lot.

2. Finish the following dialogue according to the Chinese.

提示:Alice 的母亲病了,她去学校找校长请假,校长问她请多长时间假,有什么要帮忙的,并让她写了假条。

Alice: Excuse me, Master. I'd like to take a few days off.

Master: ______________________?

Alice: My mother is ill. I have to take care of her.

Master: Oh, dear. I am sorry to hear that. ______?

Alice: No, thank you. The doctor says my mother has to be in hospital for a few days. I would like to be with her.

Master: I understand. ______________________?

Alice: I hope to be back next Monday.

Master: That's all right. ______________.

Alice: Thank you, Master. I'll write a note for permission immediately.

Master: ______________. I'll help you with your lesson later.

Culture Corner

美国孩子的请假条

美国人喜欢培养孩子的想象力,这种培养方式千奇百怪,以至于孩子们的想象力可以体现在生活中的每一个环节和细节中。比如,孩子们写出来的请假条,也充满想象力。

也许有人会以“撒谎”来非议这些想象力。但“撒谎”和想象力是不同的认知领域,它们之间是有区别的,就好像戈培尔的撒谎和海涅的想象力的区别在于精神和灵魂诉求的价值取向完全不一样。

以下是一位教师收集了当年在美国教中文时遇到的一些孩子的请假条,请大家一览:

（一）

亲爱的老师：我的外婆因为太老了，喝咖啡喝多了，神奇地从楼上掉了下来，幸好，我的外婆没有事。但我的妈妈被从掉下楼梯的外婆给砸晕过去了，现在还躺在医院。而我的父亲，那个可怜的男人还不知道这一切事情是如何发生的，竟然傻待在医院里不知所措。所以，照顾外婆和妈妈的任务就落在了我的头上。很可惜的是，我妹妹才三岁，她不能照顾我的家人，而更令人感觉糟糕的是，我还要在照顾大人的时候，照顾这个烦透了的小家伙。

（二）

亲爱的老师：你知道什么叫可怕吗？因为我家住在离城较远的地方，结果昨天晚上，我家进了狼。狼，哦，上帝，我希望老师你能同情我。狼进入家庭那可不是很普通的事情，所以，我被狼吓晕了。我妈妈很惊悚地尖叫着，可是帮不了任何忙。最后，我那个伟大的父亲竟然把我抓起来扔向了狼。所以，我受伤了，狼也受伤了。我住进了医院，狼被送到了哪里，我到现在还不知道。真同情那只狼……

（三）

亲爱的老师：世界上还有比我更倒霉的人吗？老师，我家的炉子着火了，很不幸，我就住在炉子着火的隔壁房间。于是，我被烟呛着了。可是，我还是很勇敢地帮妈妈叫了火警。值得庆幸的是，他们把我家的火浇灭了，但是我感冒了。

（四）

亲爱的老师：我不能去学校上课了，只好写请假条请安妮帮忙转达给您。我的小狗昨天很淘气，它吃光了我的作业本。结果它撑死掉了，我因为难过，今天不得不给它置办一个丧事。如果老师您愿意，也可以参加。

（五）

亲爱的老师：我家楼上有一个孩子因为洗澡忘记关水龙头，结果水从地板淋到睡在下面的我身上，现在我正躺在医院里，不是感冒了，不是生病，老师，是因为那洗澡水实在太脏了，我被臭晕了。

（六）

亲爱的老师：我哥哥昨天和我打架，他一生气把我的作业本扔出了窗外，我一时着急，跳出窗外去追我的作业本。不幸的是，作业本被风吹跑了，可是我却意外地从三楼掉到了一楼，很平安，只是擦破了一点点皮。

（七）

亲爱的老师：昨天刮台风了，您知道，对不对？好在我的体重比较大，风没有把我吹跑，可是把我骨瘦如柴的妈妈吹跑了，我为了追到她，竟然跑过了49个街道。最后，我把她从电线杆上抓下来。我妈已经昏过去。

（八）

亲爱的老师：我妈妈昨天喝醉了，她错把我当成了爸爸，结果昨天晚上，她把我骂得狗血喷头，我被她的口水淋到要死。非常抱歉，我今天还没有洗干净，总觉得全身都是她的口水味。

（九）

亲爱的老师：我昨天梦见上帝告诉我，今天不能去上学，否则会被你骂，所以，我只好请假了。

（十）

我很遗憾地告诉您，我儿子今天不能去上课了。因为他的背包昨天在乘地铁的时候，被夹在门缝里，因为风太大，把书包给吹破了。书全丢在了地铁道上。为了帮助儿子找回书本，我们花了将近一个晚上的时间奔走在地铁里。可怜的是，我和我儿子都生病了。因为被地铁车的轰鸣声给吓的。

（十一）

亲爱的老师：我家的花开了，真是奇怪，为什么偏偏在今天开。它们不知道我要去上学的吗？为了能如您所讲，要观察大自然，所以我只好请假在家，仔细欣赏那几朵花了。

Section 3 Bank Service

Warming-up

1. Match the words or phrases with the correct pictures.

A. deposit/withdraw	B. password	C. interest	D. passbook
E. card/account No.	F. credit card	G. exchange rate	H. identification card

a. ________________

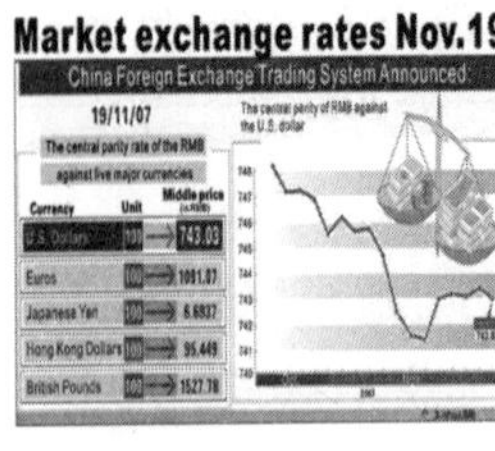

b. ________________

c. ________________

d. ________________

e. ________________

f. ________________

g. ________________

h. ________________

2. ***Work in pairs as follows.***

A: Can I help you?

B: I'd like to …

Sentence Patterns

Clerk	Customer
May I help you?	I want to open an account.
Hello, welcome to ICBC.	I'd like to apply for a credit card.
What banking services do you need?	I need to withdraw some money from my passbook.
Could I do anything for you?	I want to change the money into dollars.
What can I do for you?	Yes. Would you tell me how to deposit the money?

Communicating

Dialogue A

(The bank clerk is helping Jack deal with something in the bank.)

Clerk: Good morning! Can I help you?

Jack: Good morning! I want to open an account.

Clerk: OK. Please fill in this application form and show me your identity card.

Jack: Here it is.

Clerk: Well, here are your identity card and passbook.

Jack: Thank you. May I apply for a credit card?

Clerk: Certainly. Please fill in another form.

Jack: Thanks a lot.

Dialogue B

Clerk: What can I do for you?

Jack: Yes. I want to withdraw ¥3,000.

Clerk: Please fill in a withdrawal form.

Jack: Here you are. What's the exchange rate?

Clerk: This is the list.

Jack: Thank you. Please help me change the money into dollars.

Clerk: OK.

Vocabulary

account	[ə'kaʊnt]	*n.*	账户;解释;账目,账单;理由
passbook	['pɑːsbʊk]	*n.*	存折
withdraw	[wɪð'drɔː]	*vt.*	提;取(银行账户中的款)
exchange	[ɪks'tʃeɪndʒ]	*n.*	交换;交流;兑换
open an account			开户
fill in			填写
an application form			一张申请表
identity card			身份证
a credit card			一张信用卡
a withdrawal form			一张提款单
exchange rate			汇率;兑换率

Practice

1. Finish the following dialogue according to the Chinese.

提示:Jack 想办一张银行卡,银行职员请他填申请表,并告诉他用这个银行卡可以在任何一台柜员机存取款,Jack 出示了护照。然后填取款单并从存折账户上取了 5000 元人民币,并兑换成美元。

Clerk: Good morning. ________________?

Jack: Good morning. ____________________.

Clerk: Certainly. ________________________. You may make deposits, withdrawals at any ATM with your credit card.

Jack: Thank you.

2. Make up the rest of the dialogue according to the Chinese above.

Culture Corner

(一) 银行小常识

国内外银行的英文全称及其简称:

1. 国内银行

中国银联 China Union Pay

中国银行 BOC(Bank of China)

中国工商银行 ICBC(Industrial & Commercial Bank of China)

中国农业银行 ABOC(Agricultural Bank of China)

中国建设银行 CCB (China Construction Bank)

中国招商银行 CMB (China Merchants Bank)

交通银行 Bank of Communications

中国邮政储蓄银行 Postal Savings Bank of China

中信银行 China CITIC Bank

商业银行 Commercial Bank

农村商业银行 RCB (Rural Commercial Bank)

江苏银行 Bank of Jiangsu

南京银行 Bank of Nanjing

香港上海汇丰银行 Hong Kong and Shanghai Banking Corporation

2. 国外银行

国外银行的简称,多取第一个英文字母。

(1) 美国

美国花旗银行 Citi Bank

美国银行 Bank of America

美国纽约银行 Bank of New York Company

(2) 英国

苏格兰皇家银行 Royal Bank of Scotland

英国渣打银行 Standard Chartered Bank

(3) 法国

法国巴黎银行 BNP Paribas

(4) 日本

日本东京三菱银行 Mitsubishi Tokyo Financial Group

日本瑞穗金融集团 Mizuho Financial Group

日本三井住友银行 Sumitomo Mitsui Banking Corporation

(5) 瑞士银行 Swiss National Bank

(6) 德意志银行 Deutsche Bank

(二) 银行业务的分类

按业务复杂程度和对网点依赖程度，银行业务可分为两块：一部分是传统业务，包括一般贷款、简单外汇买卖、贸易融资等，主要是靠大量分行网络、业务量来支持。另外一部分是复杂业务，如衍生产品、结构性融资、租赁、引进战略投资者、收购兼并上市等，这些并不是非常依赖分行网络，是高技术含量、高利润的业务领域。

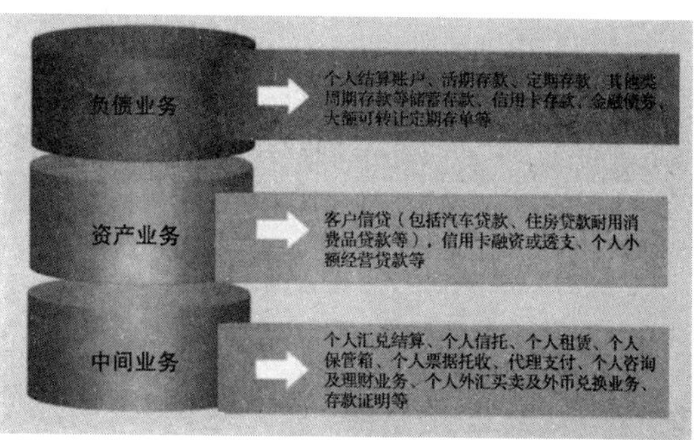

按照其资产负债表的构成，银行业务主要分为三类：负债业务、资产业务、中间业务。

1. 负债业务

负债业务是商业银行形成资金来源的业务，是商业银行中间业务和资产的重要基础。商业银行负债业务主要由存款业务、借款业务、同业业务等构成。负债是银行由于授信而承担的将以资产或资本偿付的能以货币计量的债务。存款、派生存款是银行的主要负债，约占资金来源的80%以上，另外联行存款、同业存款、借入或拆入款项或发行债券等，也构成银行的负债。

(1) 自有资金

商业银行的自有资金是指其拥有所有权的资本金。

(2) 存款负债

存款是银行负债业务中最重要的业务，是商业银行资金的主要来源。

(3) 借款负债

借款负债是商业银行通过票据的再抵押、再贴现等方法从中央银行融入资金和通过同业拆借市场向其他银行借入短期活动。

(4) 其他负债

其他负债是指商业银行利用除存款负债和借款负债以外的其他方式形成的资金来源。

2. 资产业务

资产业务是商业银行运用资金的业务,包括贷款业务、证券投资业务、现金资产业务。

(1) 储备资产

储备资产是银行为应付存款提取而保存的各种形式的支付准备金的总称。

(2) 信贷资产

信贷资产是指银行所发放的各种贷款所形成的资产业务。

(3) 投资业务

投资业务是指银行参与有价证券买卖而持有证券形成的业务。

(4) 放款业务

放款业务是商业银行最主要的资产业务。

3. 中间业务

中间业务是指不构成商业银行表内资产、表内负债形成银行非利息收入的业务,包括交易业务、清算业务、支付结算业务、银行卡业务、代理业务、托管业务、担保业务、承诺业务、理财业务、电子银行业务。

(1) 支付结算业务

支付结算类业务是指由商业银行为客户办理因债权债务关系引起的与货币支付、资金划拨有关的收费业务。

(2) 银行卡业务

银行卡是由经授权的金融机构(主要指商业银行)向社会发行的具有消费信用、转账结算、存取现金等全部或部分功能的信用支付工具。

(3) 代理业务

代理类中间业务指商业银行接受客户委托、代为办理客户指定的经济事务、提供金融服务并收取一定费用的业务,包括代理政策性银行业务、代理中国人民银行业务、代理商业银行业务、代收代付业务、代理证券业务、代理保险业务、代理其他银行银行卡收单业务等。

(4) 担保及承诺

担保类中间业务指商业银行为客户债务清偿能力提供担保,承担客户违约风险的业务。主要包括银行承兑汇票、备用信用证、各类保函等。

(5) 交易类业务

交易类中间业务指商业银行为满足客户保值或自身风险管理等方面的需要,利用各种金融工具进行的资金交易活动,主要包括金融衍生业务。

投资银行业务主要包括证券发行、承销、交易、企业重组、兼并与收购、投资分析、风险投资、项目融资等业务。

(6) 基金托管业务

基金托管业务是指有托管资格的商业银行接受基金管理公司委托，安全保管所托管的基金的全部资产，为所托管的基金办理基金资金清算款项划拨、会计核算、基金估值、监督管理人投资运作。包括封闭式证券投资基金托管业务、开放式证券投资基金托管业务和其他基金的托管业务。

(7) 咨询顾问类业务

咨询顾问类业务指商业银行依靠自身在信息、人才、信誉等方面的优势，收集和整理有关信息，并通过对这些信息以及银行和客户资金运动的记录和分析，形成系统的资料和方案，提供给客户，以满足其业务经营管理或发展的需要的服务活动。

(8) 其他中间业务

包括保管箱业务以及其他不能归入以上七类的业务。